BEYOND DISTRICT 12

THE STARS OF THE HUNGER GAMES

JENNIFER LAWRENCE

JOSH HUTCHERSON

LIAM HEMSWORTH

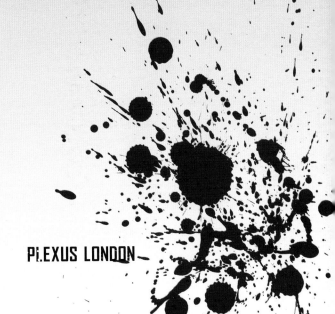

PLEXUS LONDON

CONTENTS

INTRODUCTION

In an unspecified future time, North America has been ravaged by an apocalypse, and a new autocratic nation has risen up out of the smouldering ashes of the former continental United States of America.

Panem, which consists of a fabulously wealthy Capitol and twelve far less opulent satellite 'districts', lies somewhere within the sprawling 3,000-mile stretch of mountains that Americans had called the 'Rocky Mountains'. But, ruled by systematic oppression and exploitation, the half-starved inhabitants scratching a living within the twelve subjugated districts have no knowledge or understanding of what life was like for their long-forgotten American forebears. While Panem's wealthiest and most powerful citizens live in opulent grandeur in the high-tech Capitol, the citizens of the districts live in servitude catering to the Capitol's needs.

Though it is never spoken about, there had once been a thirteenth district, supposedly destroyed in retribution for its unruly populace, who dared to rise up in rebellion against the Capitol.

To keep the masses in their subservient place, each and every year, during an event known as the 'reaping', two adolescents – one boy and one girl between the ages of twelve and eighteen – are selected by lottery from each of the twelve districts and taken to the Capitol, where they are forced to participate in the Hunger Games.

Opposite: *Jennifer Lawrence shows off her newly brunette locks outside* The Late Show with David Letterman *in 2011.*

Above: *Jennifer debuts as Katniss on the May 2011 cover of* Entertainment Weekly.

'I had read the books before I even knew I would be auditioning for the movie, and was a huge fan of the material. I feel like a fan that gets to dress up.'
– Jennifer Lawrence

Like the gladiatorial contests fought within Ancient Rome's Coliseum, Panem's Hunger Games have come to be regarded as the highlight of the Capitol's social calendar, with the high and mighty attending the contests dressed in their finery. The Games are also televised on giant screens throughout the twelve districts, and everyone living within the districts is required to watch the proceedings. Two tributes representing their particular district – who could well be their own sons, daughters, nieces or nephews – are pitted against each other and mutated beasts in a fight to the death, fought in a specially-constructed outdoor arena.

The Games are also compulsive viewing within the twelve districts because, following a victory rally, the winning tribute returns home to live in a special area of their district called the Victor's Village, where houses are well furnished and fully supplied with food. After six months, the victor then embarks on a tour of the other districts – a cruel tactic devised by the Capitol to keep the memory of the Games fresh in everyone's minds.

The glitzy, post-apocalyptic contests depicted in *The Hunger Games* are, of course, the fancies of author Suzanne Collins's imagination. But when

Opposite: *Josh Hutcherson brings old-school style to the 83rd Academy Awards in his bow-tie and tux.*

'While I was reading the books, my mind was being blown as to how much I felt like I was like Peeta, and how I felt like I could relate.'
– *Josh Hutcherson*

'I read the script, and Gale definitely felt more right than Peeta.'

– Liam Hemsworth

Lionsgate Entertainment acquired the rights for a $75-million adaptation of Suzanne's multi-million-selling *Hunger Games* trilogy, and auditions for the choice roles of Katniss Everdeen, Peeta Mellark, and Katniss's childhood friend, Gale Hawthorne (who completes the love triangle at the heart of the story), were held in April 2011, a multitude of aspiring young actors and actresses came stampeding into Hollywood, each determined to stake their claim.

Above: *Josh and Liam pose as Peeta and Gale for the August 2011 cover of* EW.

By the end of the audition process – in many ways a competition every bit as cut-throat as the Hunger Games themselves – only two boys and one girl would remain.

Rising stars Jennifer Lawrence, Josh Hutcherson and Liam Hemsworth proved that the odds most certainly were in their favour when they won the three most coveted teen roles in Hollywood: gutsy Katniss and the boys in her life, Gale and Peeta.

Opposite: *Liam Hemsworth looks sharp at the premiere of* Thor *in May 2011; the film stars his older brother, Chris.*

KATNISS EVERDEEN
THE GIRL ON FIRE

Hollywood has never been very good at keeping secrets, and celebrity gossip columnists were already hinting as much when Lionsgate announced that twenty-one-year-old Jennifer Lawrence had been chosen to play the role of Katniss Everdeen. In little over a calendar year, Kentucky-born Jennifer had gone from being a relatively fresh-faced unknown to Hollywood's next big thing, following her Best Actress Oscar-nomination for her performance as reluctant teen heroine Ree Dolly in the 2010 film *Winter's Bone*. 'I had read the books before I even knew I would be auditioning for the movie, and was a huge fan of the material. I feel like a fan that gets to dress up,' Jennifer told *Vanity Fair*. 'Actually, my mom read them first and thought it was an incredible role and story. She did the same thing with *Winter's Bone*, so she must be a clairvoyant, or just has really great taste.'

With *The Hunger Games* trilogy having sold millions of copies around the world, there was a growing legion of 'Katnissettes' all eagerly following the audition process. Yet, while many rejoiced at the news of Jennifer's appointment, there were those who thought that, at twenty-one, she was too old for the part of their teenage heroine; that her hair was the wrong colour, or that her eyes weren't the correct shade of grey. Jennifer, however, simply shrugged off the complaints: 'It was funny because everyone was upset that I was blonde, and I was like, "I'm gonna dye it." I wasn't [even] aware that everybody was so upset until after I got my hair dyed, and people were like, "Oh my gosh, blonde hair can turn brown. Wow. It's a miracle." So now is the only time that I'm being told that people hated me at first?'

***Opposite:** Eighteen-year-old Jennifer Lawrence looks every inch the silver-screen siren in an elegant blue silk dress as she attends the 65th Venice Biennale.*

THE GIRL MOST LIKELY TO ...

> 'There are actresses who build themselves, and then there are actresses who are built by others. I want to build myself.'
> – *Jennifer Lawrence*

Jennifer Shrader Lawrence, who describes herself as a 'fiery Leo', was born on 15 August 1990, and is the only girl to be born on the Lawrence side of the family in over fifty years. She and her two older brothers, Ben and Blaine, were raised on the Lawrence family farm in Shelby County, a leafy suburb of Louisville, Kentucky. But just because she was the first Lawrence to wear pink in a half-century, it didn't mean she received any special treatment from her brothers. 'Being the youngest and the only girl, I think everyone was so worried about me being a brat that they went in the exact opposite direction of treating me like Cinderella,' she subsequently told *Elle* magazine. 'I'd slap my brother on the arm, and he'd throw me down the stairs. I was always like, "Can we talk about excessive force, please?"'

Though the Lawrence clan lived on a farm, it was for residential rather than agricultural purposes, as her mother Karen ran a Shelby County children's day camp, while her father Gary owned a construction company before electing to help his wife with the day camp. During the holidays, Jennifer, or 'Jen' as she was known to the rest of the family, was often co-opted to help out around the camp, and would sort the kids out into teams for games of field-hockey, or softball. And she was happy to give cheerleading lessons to any little 'campettes' who didn't want to play sports, so they could still be involved.

Opposite: Jennifer smiles for the cameras at a Burning Plain photo call during the 65th Venice Film Festival in August 2008.

Jennifer, who has since gone on record saying that she has never taken drama classes or acting lessons and simply relies on her instincts when playing a role, first got the acting bug whilst attending Kammerer Middle School, where she helped out in various plays staged at her local church, which led to her spending a semester at the nearby Walden Theatre. By the age of fourteen, she had decided she wanted nothing more out of life than to be an actress.

In the spring of 2004 – having had the confidence to set up an audition with a talent agency in New York – Jennifer cajoled her bemused mother into taking her to the Big Apple. This was certainly a bold move on Jennifer's part, for while she knew her way around the church hall's stage, she had no formal training, or any real acting experience. Over the years, Broadway's unfeeling sidewalks have borne silent witness to countless shattered dreams, and soaked up many a tear, but Jennifer remained undaunted. And with her mother at her side, she took a deep breath and stepped through the agency's door into her future.

'Even as far back as when I started acting at fourteen, I know I've never considered failure.'
– *Jennifer Lawrence*

It seems that aside from bags of determination, Jennifer also possessed more than a modicum of acting ability, as the agency was bowled over by her professionalism. 'They told me it was the best cold read they'd ever heard from a fourteen-year-old. My mom told me they were lying,' she later jokingly recalled. 'My parents were the exact opposite of stage parents. They did everything in their power to keep it from happening. But it was going to happen no matter what. I was like, "Thanks for raising me, but I'm going to take it from here."'

Though Karen was no doubt thrilled that the agency had recognised her daughter's talents, she was rather less enthusiastic when they suggested that Jennifer should spend the summer in Manhattan to nurture said talents. It wasn't that she would ever stand in Jennifer's way, but her daughter was still only fourteen, and there was her education to think about. But fate's fickle hand was already at play,

Opposite: Jennifer looks fresh as a daisy while attending Teen Vogue's *annual Young Hollywood party in 2008.*

'My parents were the exact opposite of stage parents. They did everything in their power to keep it from happening.'
– *Jennifer Lawrence*

Above: Jennifer attends Movieguide*'s Faith and Values Awards in February 2007.*

'I'm not always right. I'm a good listener, and I'm open to being told I'm wrong.'
– *Jennifer Lawrence*

and, on leaving the agency, Jennifer was spotted by another agent who – despite being in the midst of a hectic shoot for an H&M ad – asked if he could take her picture. The agent was obviously pleased with the results, as the very next day he invited Jennifer into the studio to audition for a Reese's Peanut Butter Puff commercial. And while she didn't get the part, the agency was so impressed with Jennifer's acting abilities that they signed her up on the spot, and strongly urged Karen to allow her daughter to spend the summer in New York.

Had Jennifer been eighteen at this juncture, it's fair to say that she would have bundled her mother onto a bus bound for JFK airport and torn up her own return ticket before going off apartment hunting in the big bad city. But of course, as she was still a minor she had little option but to return to Louisville. However, having taken a nibble from the

Above: *A publicity shot for* The Bill Engvall Show. *Jennifer's sparkling performance on the TV sitcom helped launch her film career.*

Big Apple and liked the taste, returning to New York at the earliest opportunity was all Jennifer could think about. And, realising that this 'acting thing' was no passing fad, her parents gave up trying to talk her into becoming a lawyer or taking up some other sensible profession, and instead offered her a deal: she could pursue an acting career with their full blessing, but only if she graduated from high school first. That way, if things didn't work out, she could still apply to college.

This was all the incentive Jennifer needed, and she graduated from Ballard High School – attaining a 3.9 average – two years earlier than her peers. 'I never considered that I wouldn't be successful,' she says today. 'I never thought, "If acting doesn't work out I can be a doctor." The phrase "if it doesn't work out" never popped into my mind. And that dumb determination of being a naive fourteen-year-old has never left me.'

Seeing as Jennifer had done as they'd asked, her parents didn't stand in her way when she announced that she was going to spend the summer in New York. 'When I first got to New York, my feet hit the sidewalk and you'd have thought I was born and raised there,' she later recalled. 'I took over that town. None of my friends took me seriously. I came home and announced, "I'm going to move to New York," and they were like, "Okay." Then when I did, they kept waiting for me to fail and come back. But I knew I wouldn't. I was like, "I'll show you."'

With hindsight, it's not all that surprising that Jennifer's friends didn't take her seriously, as, although they knew she loved acting, her saying that she was moving to New York to become a serious actress was akin to her saying she was relocating to Paris to become a supermodel, or joining NASA to become an astronaut. Her fellow classmates at Ballard High would've no doubt been equally bemused. But whereas the majority would have been mildly envious rather than filled with jealousy, one of those who would have been really rooting for Jennifer to fall flat on her face was a girl called Meredith, whom Jennifer subsequently described as her 'childhood nemesis'. Apparently Meredith's loathing for Jennifer knew no bounds. She

'Teenagers only have to focus on themselves – it's not until we get older that we realise that other people exist.'
– Jennifer Lawrence

once asked her to hand out a stack of invitations to her birthday party, whilst purposely omitting Jennifer from the guest-list. 'Who does that?' Jennifer asked when recalling the incident years later, clearly still amazed at the other girl's callousness. 'You're just outing yourself as mean. Even the Nazis didn't do what they did simply to be evil.' She chuckled. 'I'm so happy I'm comparing Meredith to a Nazi. I hope she reads this.' And what was her response at the time? 'I started whistling,' she says. 'And I walked over to the trash can and I dumped them in. Then when I had a birthday party, I invited her. I won.'

Jennifer and her mother relocated to Manhattan during the summer of 2006, but within a year her father was ready to bring them back to Louisville. 'That was a rough time,' she told a fan website. 'During that first year in New York, my dad wanted me to come home, my mom wanted me to stay, and it was the first time I ever heard them fight. I just felt I had to get a part so they could see that this was worth it.'

Her first acting role was for MTV's *My Super Sweet 16*, which she followed with roles in TV commercials for Burger King and

Opposite: Looking stylish in black silk, Jennifer attends the premiere of The Poker House *in 2008.*

Above: *With co-star J.D. Pardo in 2008's* The Burning Plain. *Jennifer's powerful performance earned her the Marcello Mastroianni Award for best new actress at the Venice Film Festival.*

Verizon Wireless amongst others. While this was hardly a starring role in long-running smash comedy *Friends*, her namesake Jennifer Aniston had started out by appearing in TV commercials. And seeing Jennifer on TV would have surely wiped the smirks from the faces of her detractors back in Louisville.

However, her first 'real' acting break came the following year, when she was cast in the TBS comedy *The Bill Engvall Show*, which ran for three successful seasons. The show – written and created by Bill Engvall and Michael Leeson – was set in a Denver suburb and followed the life of Bill Pearson (played by Engvall), a family counsellor whose own family could use a little dose of counselling. Jennifer played Lauren, the eldest – and most mischievous – of Engvall's on-screen children. Not only did her character prove popular with viewers, but Jennifer also picked up a Young Artist Award for her endeavours.

Jennifer also made appearances in other TV shows such as *Cold Case*, *Medium*, and *Monk*, as well as getting a bit-part in a made-for-TV movie called *Company Town*. But it was undoubtedly her sparkling performances in *The Bill Engvall Show* that led to her first big-screen role, when she played Tiff in the 2008 movie *Garden Party*, which was directed by Jason Freeland and starred Vinessa Shaw and Willa Holland. And while this was another typical, blink-and-you-might-miss-her role, that same year she appeared as Agnes in actress-turned-director Lori Petty's directorial debut *The Poker House* (which earned her the Outstanding Performance Award from the Los Angeles Film Festival), as well as Guillermo Arriaga's directorial debut *The Burning Plain*.

Above: *Jennifer poses with Charlize Theron at the LA premiere of* The Burning Plain.

The Burning Plain, with its two-tiered storyline, is set during the mid-nineties, in a small town close to the Mexican border. Jennifer's character, Mariana, discovers that her mother Gina (Kim Basinger) is having an affair with a local man named Nick Martinez. In a foolhardy effort to make her mother and her lover see the error of their ways, she disassembles the gas pipe that leads into Martinez's trailer, accidentally causing an explosion that kills them. After the funeral, Mariana embarks on a relationship with Martinez's teenage son, and on discovering she is pregnant, the two flee across the border into Mexico. However, shortly after giving birth to a baby girl, Mariana abandons her new family and assumes a new identity.

Jennifer's gritty performance as Mariana subsequently earned her the Marcello Mastroianni Award for Best Young Emerging Actor/Actress during the 2008 Venice Film Festival. 'That was so fun because my family and I, at the time, had never been to Europe. And so we went for two weeks before and travelled around,' she later recalled.

OZARKS AND OSCARS

'I've always been kinda slightly schizophrenic, so I've always
kinda expected it to show up in my work. And it has.'
– *Jennifer Lawrence*

While winning the prestigious Marcello Mastroianni Award
certainly gave Jennifer plenty of kudos within the Los
Angeles acting community, her 'breakout performance' came in
Debra Granik's *Winter's Bone*, which earned her rave reviews from
prominent critics such as Roger Ebert and *New York* magazine's David
Edelstein. Indeed, such was her magnetism on screen that the *New
Yorker*'s David Denby went so far as to opine that the film would be
'unimaginable with anyone less charismatic playing Ree'.

In *Winter's Bone*, Jennifer plays seventeen-year-old Ree Dolly, who
looks after her catatonic mother; her brother, Sonny (twelve); and
her sister, Ashlee (six) in the rural Ozarks of southern Missouri. Her
wastrel of a father Jessup Dolly, a chronic meth addict, hasn't been
home for years and his whereabouts are unknown. But she's horrified
when the local sheriff arrives to tell her that if her father – who is
apparently out on bail following a drug arrest – doesn't show up for
his court date, the family will lose their home, as Jessup has put the
house and land up as part of his bond. Ree then sets out to find
Jessup, which leads her into a world where meth use is common,
violence is frequent, women are scared of their men, and people are
bound by codes of loyalty and secrecy.

'I'd have walked on hot coals to get the part. I thought it was the best

*Opposite: Lady in red: Jennifer heats up the red carpet at the 83rd Academy
Awards, where she was nominated for her part in 2010's* Winter's Bone.

female role I'd read – ever,' Jennifer later said. 'I was so impressed by Ree's tenacity and that she didn't take no for an answer. For the audition, I had to fly on the red-eye to New York and be as ugly as possible. I didn't wash my hair for a week, I had no make-up on. I looked beat up in there. I think I had icicles hanging from my eyebrows. It wasn't a fun, easy movie to make by any means. But I didn't do it to have fun.'

The role required Jennifer to learn a multitude of outdoor skills, including how to skin a squirrel. 'I should say it [the dead squirrel] wasn't real, for PETA. But screw PETA.'

When asked about the poverty she saw whilst filming in the Ozarks, she was equally blunt: 'I never felt sorry for the people. Those are their homes and their families. They probably feel sorry for us

'I'd have walked on hot coals to get the part. I thought it was the best female role I'd read – ever.'
– Jennifer Lawrence

because we don't have dinner with our family every night. And yes, there are men in our movie who say things like, "I told you to shut up once, with my mouth." But there are men in this city who say, "I'll be spending the night at the office," and they'll be sleeping with their secretaries. It's different, but it's the same.

'I grew up in Kentucky, but I did not grow up like that. I had heat, and I didn't have to shoot my dinner or anything. I wanted to be a doctor when I was little, so I'm okay with blood and guts. [But] I had to learn how to chop wood – I don't think my dad would have let me go chop wood in the backyard growing up.'

As Ree Dolly would go out hunting with a shotgun she called on help from another family member. 'My cousin cleaned out a shotgun for me and let me carry it around the house, because he said anybody who knows anything about guns is going to know in a second if someone has held a gun before. I didn't want to be that person. I wanted to be practiced.'

While *Winter's Bone* picked up both the Grand Jury Prize: Dramatic

Opposite: Survival of the fittest: Jennifer's gritty performance in Winter's Bone *signalled her arrival into the Hollywood big leagues.*

'I have this feeling of protectiveness over characters I want to play. I worry about them – if someone else gets the part, I'm afraid they won't do it right.'
– *Jennifer Lawrence*

Film Award at the 2010 Sundance Film Festival, and the Waldo Salt Screenwriting Award, Jennifer herself received Best Actress nominations at the 2010 Golden Globes, as well as the 2011 Oscars. And whilst most actors will happily tell you how they've had to suffer for their art when preparing for certain films, this wasn't the case with Jen. When she was asked how she prepared for the role of Ree, she simply said: 'To you, it looks emotionally straining, but I don't get emotionally drained because I don't invest any of my real emotions. I don't even take it to craft services [the on-set caterers].'

Jennifer is the second-youngest person to date to receive a nomination in the Best Actress category in the Academy of Motion Picture Arts and Sciences history. (Only Keisha Castle-Hughes, nominated for her 2002 performance in *Whale Rider*, was younger.)

For some Hollywood pundits, Jennifer was a safe bet for the Best Actress Oscar. 'Lawrence is as sure a thing as any other when it comes to potential Best Actress nominees,' opined *Movieline*'s editor, S.T. VanAirsdale. 'Her film has been in the critical and industry conversation for nearly a year now; she's had too long and too powerful an Oscar buzz to shake it now.'

Melena Ryzik, who covers the film awards season for the *New York Times*, and its *Carpetbagger* blog was of a similar opinion: 'Lawrence is the kind of actress people want to like. [*Winter's Bone*] is such a gritty movie, and her performance is so unvarnished. It's against type for a pretty young actress, which is what the industry likes.' While *New York* magazine's Lane Brown believed Jennifer had become such a critical favourite that a snub from the Academy would result in 'a bit of an outcry'. 'I can't think of many other snubs that would have people more upset,' she added.

Louisville doesn't have many claims to fame, so the local paper, the *Louisville Courier-Journal*, was naturally very excited at the prospect of Jennifer picking up a Best Actress Oscar. After eulogising about Jennifer's 'year-long magic red-carpet ride [which] will either come to an end — or ascend to entirely new heights', and how her performance in *Winter's Bone* was 'among the most acclaimed of last year', and earned her Best Actress nominations from the Golden

Opposite: Oscar Nominee: Jennifer gets Academy approval for her role in 2010's Winter's Bone.

Globes, the Screen Actors Guild and the Film Independent Spirit Awards, the paper carried the transcript from a telephone interview with her mother Karen, which took place when she and Gary were in Los Angeles visiting their daughter.

According to Karen, who was now helping Jennifer choose which roles to audition for, her daughter was taking it all in her relaxed stride.

> **'When you don't have anybody to take care of you, you could do whatever you want, or you could take charge and be your own parent.'**
>
> *– Jennifer Lawrence*

'She doesn't talk about it and I never talk about it. She asked me to never bring it up, so I don't,' she said. 'I'm sure she'd be thrilled and honoured, but there are just some heavy hitters in her category. The thing we're most proud of is when we go on set with these people who are around her eighteen hours a day. They see who she really is – they say she's gracious, down-to-earth.'

Jennifer's siblings, Ben and Blaine, who both still live in Louisville, have noticed a few more stares on those occasions when their famous kid sister pays them a visit. 'We've had a few strangers appear over the past few years, but it's all been supportive,' said twenty-nine-year-old Ben, who works in web design and video production for Louisville Geek. 'The funny thing is she gets noticed more in public when we're in LA than she does here in Louisville, so she loves that.'

Jennifer also loves her music, and so one of her stand-out memories from the Oscars ceremony was the entertainment: 'I was really excited because Florence and the Machine were playing,' she said in a recent interview with the *Washington Post*. 'I really remember that performance really well. It was great. I loved being able to sit next to my dad. We just kept looking at each other like, "I can't believe this is happening."'

Like every other glossy on the magazine stand, *Elle* was at the Kodak Theatre to cover the Oscars. Having described Jennifer's performance as Ree Dolly as both 'unsentimental' and 'exquisite', their reviewer went on to say that as Jennifer had gone without a trace of make-up – except for some convincing bruises – while peering out from under a low wool cap, it had almost passed unnoticed that she

Above: Jennifer looks the picture of elegance at an LA screening of Winter's Bone *in May 2010.*

was stunning, with a 'cherubic, translucent face suggesting a tweeny softness that belies an old-dame brawn and wicked wit rare among Hollywood ingénues'.

Indeed, with her tumbling blonde locks and exquisite bone structure giving her a passing resemblance to the *Dr No*-era Ursula Andress, and a husky, seductive voice that sets male pulses racing, it was inevitable that she caused a stir at the Oscars. And while she is enjoying every minute of the attention following her arrival on Tinseltown's radar, Jennifer has no intention of playing the innocent ingénue either up on the screen or in her day-to-day life. But even in the run-up to the Oscars ceremony she was going around joking about having practiced her losing face in the mirror: 'I can't wait to use it. [But] if I win, I won't be able to!'

Unlike nearly every other ingénue in Hollywood, Jennifer has no intention of catering to the film industry's whim that every woman should be a size zero. According to *Elle* magazine, Jennifer was wearing a red Calvin Klein tank-dress 'about which the phrase body-conscious would be a riotous understatement', and yet had hastily gobbled down a cheese-steak before walking up the red carpet. 'Fifteen minutes before, the guy doing my hair goes, "If you can get a salad, get a salad,"' she recalled. 'I said, "I'm getting a Philly cheese-steak." I'm sure there's proof on a hotel bill somewhere.'

Sadly for Jennifer, while she enjoyed the cheese-steak, it was her 'losing face' that she had to put on for the cameras, as both the Golden Globe and the Oscar went to Natalie Portman for her role as disturbed ballerina Nina Sayers in *Black Swan*. However, Jennifer didn't appear too disheartened when speaking to the *Louisville Courier-Journal*: 'It's an honour,' she told her hometown paper, reflecting how far she'd come in just receiving Oscar and Golden Globe nominations in the same year. 'You work so hard for something. Mostly, I'm just really happy that I've been able to do what I love. I know that sounds kind of simple, but I've found something I really love doing and I can do it every day of my life. That's what I'm most excited about. The recognition and the parties are great, but I'm mostly just excited to be here working.'

'I like when things are hard; I'm very competitive. If something seems difficult or impossible, it interests me.'
– Jennifer Lawrence

In 2009, Jennifer appeared in Jodie Foster's dark comedy *The Beaver*, in which the Oscar-winning actress-turned-director also starred alongside Mel Gibson. *The Beaver* follows Walter Black, a depressed CEO of a toy company (played by Gibson) who dons a beaver hand-puppet to better communicate with his wife Meredith (Foster), and their two sons. Jennifer played the role of Norah, the girlfriend of Porter Black (Anton Yelchin). But even when Jennifer is playing vulnerable on-screen (Norah is a valedictorian with a painful past), she still exudes a formidable, ever-so-subtle defiance. 'She finds strength in every moment,' Anton told *Elle* magazine in 2011 after playing alongside Jennifer for a second time in the film *Like Crazy*, in which she portrays a girl whose boyfriend is pining for his ex. 'I've watched her do two characters that are different, but they both have Jen in them, which is dignified. Even if they're broken, they're never weak.'

Opposite: *Jennifer as Norah in 2011's* The Beaver. *Director (and co-star) Jodie Foster was so impressed with Jen's audition that she rewrote the part to accommodate her.*

'Anytime you're away from your home filming, it messes with your head.'
– *Jennifer Lawrence*

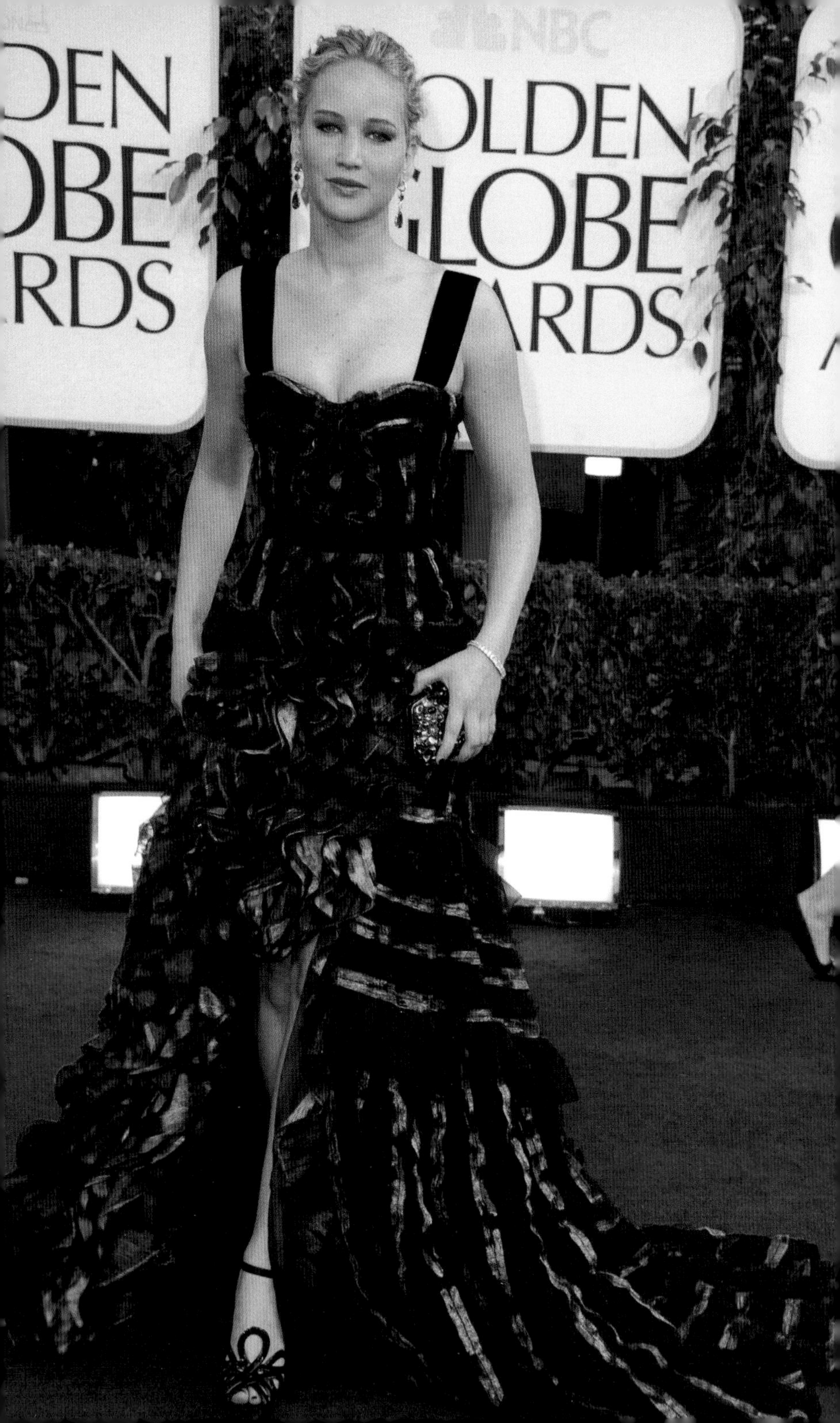
DEN
OBE
RDS
NBC
OLDEN
LOBE
ARDS

> '**The parties are great, but I'm mostly just excited to be here working.**'
> – *Jennifer Lawrence*

Little could Jennifer have known that the film would be put on hold for two years, owing to the controversies that subsequently engulfed Gibson after he was accused of assaulting a former girlfriend. However, the chance to work with Jodie Foster more than made up for the disappointment of seeing her on-screen efforts shelved. 'We both walked away thinking the same thing: "I've never met anybody who reminds me of me more,"' she said when asked about her time on set with

Above: In the bittersweet story of young love, Like Crazy, *in 2011.*

Foster. 'As far as methods go, neither of us have one. Like me, she doesn't take any of it to heart. We both think of this as a job, and don't understand why you suddenly have to become an asshole when you become successful at it. We're both perfectly fine with technical directions: "Hunch your shoulders more, lift your head up higher." And we both hate bullshit directing, like, "Imagine your puppy just died." If you want me to cry, just say cry.'

2009 also saw Jennifer appear in James Oakley's *Devil You Know*, another two-tiered story in which she plays the young Zoe Vale (with the older Zoe played by ex-Bond girl Rosamund Pike), whose mother Kathryn (Lena Olin) is a reclusive ex-movie star drawn into a web of blackmail and deceit.

Opposite: Stepping out: Jennifer cuts a striking figure at the 2011 Golden Globes.

AS RADIANT AS THE SUN

'I'm excited to be seen as sexy. But not slutty.'
– *Jennifer Lawrence*

After seemingly endless debate and speculation, *MTV News* claimed to have received 'exclusive confirmation' that Jennifer had landed the highly-coveted role of Katniss Everdeen in Lionsgate's big-screen adaptation of *The Hunger Games*. According to a Lionsgate insider, Jennifer was a fitting choice due to her 'meteoric ascent to Hollywood stardom starting with her Oscar-nominated role in *Winter's Bone*, as well as roles in Jodie Foster's *The Beaver* and Matthew Vaughn's *X Men: First Class*.'

Jennifer subsequently said of the auditions: 'I auditioned, which was a long process and a lot of improvisation. And then waited a month or something, where I was convinced I didn't have it . . . then I got the phone call while I was in London. I was then terrified. I knew it was going to be huge, and that's scary. I called my mom. She said, "This is a script that you love, and you're thinking about not doing it because of the size of it?" And I [didn't] want to not do something because I'm scared, so I said yes. And I'm so happy that I did.'

Director Gary Ross was full of praise for his lead actress: 'I'm so excited to work with Jen and see her bring this character to life. Katniss requires a young actress with strength, depth, complexity, tenderness, and power. There are very few people alive who can bring that to a role. Jen brings it in spades. She's going to be an amazing Katniss.'

Opposite: Bold and beautiful: Jennifer brightens up the red carpet in a hot-pink gown at the 2011 SAG Awards.

Above: *A delighted Jennifer accepts the Rising Star award at the Palm Springs International Film Festival.*

Jennifer described herself a 'massive fan' of *The Hunger Games* trilogy, and says she understands the fans' excitement and dedication to her Katniss Everdeen character. 'I was a cheerleader for six years, but I also have this totally competitive side. I'll wrestle anyone at any time . . . I was the manliest cheerleader. I had the lowest voice,' she told *Teen Vogue* in April 2011. 'Sometimes I get anxiety about not staying up late enough. I'm not the one in the corner, but if anyone was like, "I want to go home and watch *The Big Lebowski* [a 1998 film starring Jeff Bridges and John Goodman]," I'd be right there with my hand up.

'I have a huge responsibility to the fans of this incredible book and I don't take it lightly. I will give everything I have to these movies and to this role to make it worthy of Suzanne Collins's masterpiece.'

'So many people – after they've seen my movies – expect me to be intense and dark, and I'm not at all.'
– *Jennifer Lawrence*

Above: Jennifer brings a little Hollywood glamour to Paris Fashion Week in 2011.

Comparisons between *The Hunger Games* and *Twilight* were only to be expected, but while Jennifer readily agreed that fans of *Twilight* would enjoy *The Hunger Games*, as both sagas are popular books with large fan bases, with a 'reach' that is 'very similar', she would prefer it if the comparisons stop before they grow too loud. '*The Hunger Games* is not *Twilight*,' she recently said in *Vanity Fair*. 'It's really premature to say that it will be the same phenomenon. I'm so proud of the work we did on the film. Gary Ross and the entire cast and crew were amazing, and I can't wait for it to be brought to life because I think it's an important story. If it does become a crazy phenomenon, I'll soak up my freedom now!

'Whenever I really want a part, I'm not sure what to do. How do I let the director know how obsessed I am and willing to do anything for the movie? Like, I wanted to write this one director a letter, so I wrote him a handwritten note. But then I was like, "How many people are writing this guy handwritten letters?" Is it going to seem cheesy? What do I do? Do I sleep outside of his house until he agrees to give me the part?'

2011 proved to be a busy year for Jennifer, for aside from landing the much-coveted role of Katniss in *The Hunger Games*, she co-starred in the aforementioned independent film *Like Crazy*, as well as landing the role of Raven Darkholme/Mystique, the shape-shifting villainess in *X-Men: First Class*, a prequel to the highly successful *X-Men* franchise, starring Michael Fassbender as Magneto, and James McAvoy as Professor Charles Xavier (the roles made famous by Sir Ian McKellen and Patrick Stewart).

In the prequel, which is set against the backdrop of the Cuban Missile Crisis of May 1963, the homeless young shape-shifter Raven is befriended by telepath Xavier in New York. Xavier is overjoyed to meet someone else who is 'different', and invites Raven to live with him and his family in England. Whilst seeking Xavier's advice on mutation, CIA agent Moira MacTaggert (Rose Byrne), convinces him

> **'Making movies isn't a choice for me; I have to make movies because I love acting. And when I'm on set, I'm just thinking about the script and of working.'**
> *– Jennifer Lawrence*

and Raven – who by this time has adopted the name Mystique – to join her at the CIA's secret Division X, so as to convince the CIA's sceptical director that mutants really do exist. Whilst there they meet a young scientist called Hank McCoy (Nicholas Hoult), who is a prehensile-footed mutant. McCoy develops a bond with Raven and promises her that he will find a way to normalise their appearance. However, the megalomaniacal Magneto succeeds in convincing Mystique to embrace her nature as a mutant and join him.

'Fox wanted me for *X-Men* and I knew I needed to talk to my mom. She just wanted to make sure I was doing it for the right reasons, and I told her I didn't know,' Jennifer subsequently revealed in an interview on *The Hunger Games* website. 'Eventually I read the script – which they were guarding like it was the Holy Grail – and I think I was preparing for the script to be bad. Later in the process I read the script and it was actually really good. And it was going to star two of my favourite actors, Michael Fassbender and James McAvoy. So those were the things I loved, and they were intriguing. But at the

Opposite above: First Class: Jennifer as the shape-shifting femme fatale, Mystique, in the 2011 X-Men prequel. **Opposite below:** *Mystique in her 'mutant form'.*

'I have a huge responsibility to the fans of this incredible book and I don't take it lightly. I will give everything I have to these movies and to this role to make it worthy of Suzanne Collins's masterpiece.'
– *Jennifer Lawrence*

time there was no script and nothing to really go by. And with *X-Men*, there would be sequels involved.'

Sequels weren't very high on her agenda, as she explained: 'It's hard to talk about a movie to do when there are sequels and you haven't read the script, because what if I hate the script and I have to make it three times? So I think the sequels were the biggest thing for me, because I was thinking that I have no idea where I'm going to be in my life when these new movies come out. I don't know what kind of things I'm going to be doing. Am I going to regret this decision I made when I was twenty? So I wanted to really think about it.'

Jennifer's Mystique is, of course, a younger version of the character played by Rebecca Romijn in the earlier *X-Men* films. 'For the most part, doing a prequel is great because you do have room to kind of free this character and how they got to where they are instead of being a slave to exactly what the previous actor [Romijn] did.'

Jennifer, who would subsequently confess to never having seen any of the *X-Men* films prior to her audition, says that only ten percent of her screen time will be as Mystique, as it takes the make-up artists an average of six painstaking hours to transform her into the character. She jokingly told reporters that blue body paint smelt so bad that she took to calling herself 'Mystink' whenever she was due for make-up. 'Nothing's sacred anymore,' she continued. 'Those girls and I got so close. They were painting me naked every day for months. It was kind of like going to a really bizarre sleepover. It's what you guys imagine we do: one naked girl and seven pairs of hands all over her.'

The action-packed role required Jennifer to book a few sessions in the gym. 'For *X-Men* I was lifting a lot of weights,' she explained. 'I actually lost a lot of mass when I [finished the film] because I was working out so much and very muscular and strong. And did I feel naked being naked? Yeah. Totally.'

While Jennifer is a girl who always eats what she pleases, it was the thought of going naked save for the blue body paint that saw her submit to a gruelling twice-a-day training regimen. And this, coupled with a high-protein diet, allowed her to sculpt, yet maintain, her shapely curves. 'I knew that if I was going to be naked in front

Opposite: Looking her sultry best, Jennifer arrives at the 2011 Film Independent Spirit Awards.

of the world, I wanted to look like a woman and not a prepubescent thirteen-year-old boy,' she told *Elle* magazine. 'I'm so sick of people thinking that's what we're supposed to look like.'

And the scripted 'bond' between her and Nicholas Hoult's on-screen characters has spilled over into real life. The Hollywood rumour-mill creaked into action when Jennifer and Hoult were spotted at several after-show parties following Jennifer's appearance at the 2011 Screen Actors Guild Awards held in Los Angeles back in January. According to one 'spy-witness', they were inseparable all night, holding hands and looking incredibly cute together.

Jennifer also featured in David O. Russell's *The Silver Linings Playbook*, with Robert De Niro. In the film Jennifer plays Tiffany, a beautiful young woman whose life hasn't turned out the way she wanted. On being befriended by the film's main character Pat (Bradley

> ## 'I'm so proud of the work we did on the film. Gary Ross and the entire cast and crew were amazing.'
> ### *– Jennifer Lawrence*

Cooper), a clinically depressed former teacher who's spent the past four years in a mental institution after losing his wife to another man. Together, Pat and Tiffany try to navigate through their lives and stay true to who they are, always just one adventure away from a unique friendship, and possibly more.

It is rumoured that Jennifer beat off a host of leading actresses, including Elizabeth Banks, Kirsten Dunst, Blake Lively, Rooney Mara, Rachel McAdams, Andrea Riseborough and Olivia Wilde to land the highly-coveted role. She is also set to star alongside Elisabeth Shue in Mark Tonderai's horror-thriller *House at the End of the Street,* in which she plays a teenage girl who moves to a new neighbourhood and discovers that a double murder occurred in the house across the street. She subsequently befriends the crime's only survivor, Jumper (Max Theriot). According to the *Hollywood Reporter, House at the End of the Street* is looking 'to be to *Psycho* what *Disturbia* was to *Rear Window*'.

In a recent interview with *Flare* magazine, Jennifer surprised many of

Opposite: Girl on fire: Jennifer debuts her new 'Hunger Games hair' at The Late Show with David Letterman *in 2011.*

Above: Jennifer visits Jimmy Fallon on Late Night *to promote* X-Men: First Class.

> **'I want people to say, "I'm in a really bad mood, let's go see a Jennifer Lawrence movie."'**
> *— Jennifer Lawrence*

her fans by revealing her dislike for shopping. 'Going shopping's still not really my comfort zone. I can tell what looks pretty, and I know what designers I like wearing, and the more I learn about designers the more I'm liking it. I've worn a lot of Louis Vuitton lately and Proenza Schouler, but I still have tons from Forever 21. But I still hate shopping. To me, shopping is torture.'

However, that doesn't mean to say she doesn't like getting dolled up for awards ceremonies and other big Hollywood occasions. 'I spend so much time reading scripts and preparing [for roles] that it's nice to have all these dresses to choose from. They're all beautiful and I can't believe I get to pick.' She also revealed that she enjoyed getting 'sexy and flirty' on photo shoots. And as for her being considered a sex symbol? 'It feels weird, but not bad at all.'

Though Jennifer is very much a 21st-century girl, she regards the internet as something of a 'black hole' that is best left alone, and refuses to open a Facebook account, while Twitter is absolutely 'out of the question'. 'I think the quick fame is scarier because I don't really work a computer, so I don't ever read comments. That never really scares me, what people think. If I read it, it would scare the hell out of me, but I'm not worried about that,' she said in a recent interview with the

Washington Post. 'What does worry me is how important these things are, and I don't want to offend or disappoint anyone. It's scary, when you think of these huge fan bases behind them and you think you're holding these characters that a lot of people are going to put a lot of weight into. So, like I said, the really scary part is quick fame.'

And of course being hailed as the 'obsession of the year' and an 'It actress' does have its occasional downsides. 'I have hair and make-up people coming to my house every day and putting me in new, uncomfortable, weird dresses and expensive shoes,' she groaned. 'And I just shut down and raise my arms up for them to get the dress on, and pout my lips when they need to put the lipstick on. [In a way] that's exactly what it's like for Katniss in the Capitol. She was a girl who's all of a sudden being introduced to fame. I know what that feels like to have all this flurry around you and feel like, "Oh, no, I don't belong here."

'Yesterday I had to do an interview. I was in a horrible mood. I couldn't think of basic words. I could see my publicist in the background, mouthing things to say. They want you to be likeable all the time, and I'm just not.

'It's easy to get pigeonholed, so I think it's important that when one thing gets really big it's a wise decision to do the opposite. I have a choice of really good things, not a bad movie versus a good movie. But if I say yes to everything, I won't have a day off for, like, the next four years. I want to play a character I've never been before – a crazy serial killer like Charlize Theron in *Monster*. I'd love to have to shave my head.'

2012 looks to be an equally hectic year for Jennifer, as she's been listed as one of eight nominees for the Rising Star trophy at the British Academy Film Awards. Yet, her fans will be shocked to learn that she actually considered giving up acting in the past. 'People started talking to me differently and I couldn't stand that,' she said. 'I'd go to parties where I used to be invisible and off the record . . . now everybody's watching and listening. There was a weird element and I wondered whether I wanted to be a director or just do indie films.'

But with her name now occupying space on every Hollywood director's short-list, Jennifer had better get accustomed to the star treatment. 'When you're on set, everybody's like, "Oh, do you need water? Here's forty-five bottles!" It's really bizarre,' she says. 'I'm still getting used to it. I'm still in wonderland.'

PEETA MELLARK

THE BOY WITH THE BREAD

Lionsgate's confirmation that Jennifer's fellow Kentuckian Josh Hutcherson had landed the role of Peeta Mellark came hot on the heels of rumours that the *Bridge to Terabithia* star had been one of the front-runners during the audition process. A number of actors from Hollywood's latest 'brat pack' – including Alex Pettyfer, Lucas Till, Nico Tortorella, and Hunter Parrish – had also competed for the sought-after role. But while gossip columnists welcomed the news, as with Jennifer's casting, many fans of *The Hunger Games* trilogy questioned Josh's appointment because he didn't resemble the character described in Collins's books.

Josh, having seen first-hand what magic Hollywood's make-up artists were capable of, knew such anxieties were groundless. And despite having appeared in more than a dozen films – many of which had been starring roles – he admitted in *Vanity Fair* that he'd 'never felt more right for a character' in his whole life.

'I don't read a whole lot of books because I'm usually busy reading scripts, but these books were so good that I literally read all three of them over the course of five days or something. I really powered through them,' he enthused. 'And while I was reading the books, my mind was being blown as to how much I felt like I was like Peeta, and how I felt like I could relate. That, in a way, is kind of even more scary, because if you don't get hired, it's like, "Oh my God, what am I? What am I doing? What's wrong?"'

Opposite: *Looking cool and casual, Josh attends the 2011 Independent Spirit Awards.*

THE ONE TO WATCH

'It's not all glamour. I learned that right away.
I thought getting into acting would be a breeze, and nice
and easy. I thought, "How hard could it be?"'
– Josh Hutcherson

Joshua 'Josh' Ryan Hutcherson was born on 12 October 1992 in Union, a small rural city which lies in Boon County, on the Kentucky/Ohio border, and at the time of the 2010 census had a population of just 5,379. Josh's dad Chris is a management analyst for the EPA (Environmental Protection Agency), while his doting mother Michelle – a former emergency response trainer with Delta Airlines – gave up her job to manage Josh's career.

It seems that Josh wanted to be an actor almost from the moment he could walk and talk, as if he could already see the fun in playing someone else when most kids were still learning to be themselves. As the kids from his neighbourhood and kindergarten were busy doing their own thing, Josh called on his two imaginary friends – named 'Hamo' and 'Damo' – to serve as willing extras in his mind's-eye movies. 'I don't know why they were named Hamo and Damo, but we'd sing Barney songs together, as embarrassing as that is!' Josh sheepishly confided recently. 'I was also obsessed with Teenage Mutant Ninja Turtles when I was younger. So obsessed that every time I'd walk over a drain, I'd bend over and say, "Hi, turtles!" When I was like, five years old, I used to have really bad nightmares about the Wicked Witch of the West from *The Wizard of Oz*. In my dream, I would open my eyes and look out the window, and she would be there! I'd wake up scared to death.'

*Opposite: Young Josh is all smiles at the premiere
of* Zathura: A Space Adventure *in 2005.*

When he wasn't hiding under the bedclothes or hunched over drain covers searching for ass-kicking anthropomorphic turtles, Josh could be found entertaining his mom, dad and baby brother Connor with things he'd picked up from watching TV. 'Ever since he's been little, he's liked to perform for people,' Chris said of his son's earliest public performances. 'He has a personality that attracts people's attention. He does have talent. And it's part of a parent's responsibility, if your child wants to do something, support him whenever you can.'

'He bugged us so much,' Michelle agreed. 'He wanted to do it. I have no clue why. We just thought, "He's a kid, he doesn't know what he wants." And finally, he just pushed and pushed enough that I said I'd look into it. And I did. And this is where it went, all of a sudden.'

'I got a lot of crap from kids in school when I first started acting. I didn't understand that, because it was something I loved doing.'
– Josh Hutcherson

Josh, however, remembers things slightly differently, and said that Chris and Michelle – knowing nothing about show business or acting, and thinking it was a passing fancy – continually ignored his pleas until one fateful day in January 2002. 'I had to beg and beg my parents since I was three or four years old, and they said, "Why not play sports?" They heard all this negative stuff about Hollywood and being an actor. Finally, they opened the Yellow Pages and we met with an acting coach.'

The acting coach in question was Bob Luke, who came via the Heyman Talent Agency based in Oakley, California, but with another office in Cincinnati. Luke liked what he saw, and having recommended several Hollywood agents he knew who were always on the lookout for a 'good-looking all-American boy-next-door', suggested to Michelle that she take Josh to Los Angeles and audition for TV pilots. So she did. 'They tried me out there and suggested I go to pilot season in Los Angeles. I was so excited and begged and begged and begged, and so

Opposite: *Two thumbs up: Josh shows his approval at the 2002 premiere of* Polar Express.

'Every time I read anything, whether it be a book, a script or anything, I automatically imagine myself as the boy in the plot.'
– *Josh Hutcherson*

they took me out for one pilot season. I got a pilot, and things took off from there and never stopped. To this day, I have never had an acting class in my life.'

Like Jennifer, Josh started out appearing in TV commercials for companies such as Kellogg's, McDonald's, and Ace Hardware. Though he would miss out on film roles in *Home Alone 4*, Mike Myers's *The Cat in the Hat*, and *Bringing Down the House*, he eventually made his screen debut in *House Blend*, a Warner Bros. comedy pilot with Amy Yasbeck. He followed this by playing former Charlie's Angel Kate Jackson's son Charlie in the Animal Planet film *Miracle Dogs*, which also starred former Golden Girl Rue McClanahan, and Stacy Keach.

> **'That's kind of why I like to be an actor, because I get to play different characters and pretend I'm different people going through different situations.'**
> **– Josh Hutcherson**

Playing the loveable son came very naturally to Josh, and this was evident in the TNT made-for-TV family film, *Wilder Days*, in which Josh stars as Chris Morse, who accompanies his ailing grandfather James 'Pop Up' Morse (played by Peter Falk, best known for his role as long-running TV detective Columbo) on a road trip in a '59 Cadillac so the old man can prove that the colourful stories he'd regaled Chris with when he was younger are true. When his grandfather becomes ill, Josh gets to drive the car. 'He was tired, and he pulled over at a rest stop,' Josh recalled when asked about the film, which was shot over four weeks in Vancouver. 'I was looking around, and heard scary noises, so I got in the car and just drove away, and tried to find a hotel. Then I hit a deer. And I get out and try to bring it back to life with jumper cables, because that was one of his stories. I sat in the driver's seat, while the stunt coordinator was low down in the car, and he pressed the gas and brakes. I just steered the wheel.'

If Josh had told his peers at New Haven Elementary School back in Union that his name was on billboards in Hollywood, they would probably have dismissed this as one of his colourful stories. Yet any sceptics would've been left eating humble pie. 'I honestly started crying when I saw the billboard advertising *Wilder Days*,' Michelle told the *Cincinnati Enquirer*. 'You never imagine that one day, your eleven-year-

Above: *Josh poses with on-screen dad, Will Ferrell, at the premiere of 2005's* Kicking and Screaming.

old son will be on a billboard on Sunset Boulevard in the middle of Hollywood. Josh just started screaming when he saw it!'

Michelle, however, was desperate to keep Josh's feet firmly planted on the ground. 'We work hard to keep his life as normal as it can be. He doesn't get to just go out and buy things. His three big purchases – a dirt bike, a laptop and a gas-powered motor scooter – have been spread out over eighteen months,' she told the paper. 'Every kid around here has a motorised scooter, but he was the last kid to get one in our subdivision. We didn't let him at first. He kept working hard, and doing chores around here, so we decided to let him get one. We give him as normal of a life that we can. We let him be a kid. That's what a lot of people say to me, "He's so professional, yet he's still a kid." And I think that's because we let him be a kid.'

Above: First kiss: Josh puckers up in 2005's Little Manhattan.

And while most parents with a promising child actor in the family would have surely packed their bags and headed for Hollywood and Vine, Michelle was happy to 'do the commuting thing', while Chris stayed behind in Union looking after Connor, who has a couple of Hollywood credits of his own to his name, but says he's not really interested in following in his older brother's footsteps. 'Connor is very smart,' Josh says of his brother. '[He] wants to be a rocket scientist or something cool like that.'

'Moving to LA would mean that Chris gives up his career, and we don't want to do that,' Michelle said. 'Sometimes child actors don't have very long careers, and then we would have given up our home and Chris's career. We really like keeping our home as home, because that's where all our family is.'

2003 also saw Josh appear in the independent film *American Splendor*, which – as *Winter's Bone* would seven years later – scooped the Grand Jury Prize at the 2003 Sundance Film Festival. The following year Josh added further strings to his bow by providing the voice for the character Markl in the animated film *Howl's Moving Castle*, as well as Hero Boy in the 2004 computer-animated Christmas blockbuster, *The Polar Express*, which starred Tom Hanks. Josh loved the experience – especially being rigged in harnesses to fly through the air as young Hero Boy. (Hanks plays the adult Hero Boy.) 'I supposedly fall off a train, and grab onto the back of it, and slingshot myself back up onto some guy's shoulders, and then we fell off again,' Josh enthused.

Slowly but surely Josh was chipping away at making a name for himself in Hollywood, and 2005 saw him appear in four widely contrasting films. The first was a relatively minor role in director Tony Vitale's *One Last Ride*, which explored the struggles of a gambling addict, while later that year he played Will Ferrell's soccer son in the family comedy *Kicking and Screaming*.

'If I'm not working and I'm home then I'm always on the go playing football or going out with my friends. I don't sit still much.'
– Josh Hutcherson

In the romantic-comedy *Little Manhattan*, Josh plays ten-year-old Gabriel 'Gabe' Burton, who slowly realises that girls can actually be pretty and nice to be around. 'It was really cool because I was involved with this movie before it actually became a movie,' Josh recalled. 'They were still developing the script and everything. I was there to read with all the different girls, and I got to have my opinion on which girl. Yeah, the thing is, I said that Charlie [Ray, who played Josh's character's love interest in the film] was one of my favourites, so that was really cool. I was so shocked when I found out that was her first audition ever because she was really so good.'

It's been whispered that Josh was rather more nervous about doing his first on-screen kiss than Charlie. When Josh asked co-director Mark Levin why was it that he was so nervous when Charlie was seemingly taking it all in her stride, Levin smiled and shot Josh with a line that was used often throughout the movie: 'Well, it's because girls mature faster than boys!' he told him.

However, Josh proved infinitely more confident when it came to

Above: *Playing a dangerous game: Josh argues with his brother in the science-fiction adventure* Zathura.

other stuff. 'Josh was the first kid we met at the reading, and he so blew everyone away at the reading that he made it impossible for them to say no,' Levin enthused. 'Josh is so game for anything that you put in front of him, and he's got an amazing acting style, which is that he just is "Johnny on the spot". You just say, "Hit that window," and he says, "How hard?" And he does it again and again. And he enjoys it, he's just having fun . . . it's just kind of indicative of his incredible commitment.'

Actress Cynthia Nixon, who played Josh's on-screen mother Leslie, was equally impressed: 'Sometimes you just run across kids who are so grown-up. Josh is cute, but he is also smart and makes good choices.'

Josh's brother Connor actually makes a blink-and-you'll-miss-it

'You never imagine that your eleven-year-old son will be on a billboard on Sunset Boulevard in Hollywood.'
— Michelle Hutcherson, Josh's mother

Above: Josh with his proud parents and little brother, Connor, at the Zathura *premiere.*

appearance in *Little Manhattan*, and is credited on IMDB as 'the boy who throws up'. But of course, Connor has gone on record saying he has no interest in pursuing an acting career, and only appeared in the film because he thought it might be fun to work with his big brother.

Though Josh has enjoyed working on every film he's made to date, if he was forced to chose his favourite it would – at least up until now – be *Zathura: A Space Adventure*. 'That was awesome because of all the stunts and cool ways that they filmed it,' he enthused. 'They used three different sets. One shook like a 9.2 earthquake, one tilted at a forty-five-degree angle, and the other was still. Also, it was all in the same place so once we got there, we got to do cool stuff with the trailer for Halloween and Christmas and stuff like that. It was a lot of fun.

'I love doing roles and movies that are different from each other,' he continued. 'That's kind of why I like to be an actor, because I get to play different characters and pretend I'm different people going through different situations. Getting to do different genres of movies means you're gonna have different types of situations and stuff like that. So I want to try and do every type of genre there is out there.'

SPANNING THE BRIDGE

'I have been surprised by how hard [filming] can be. When you get into it you don't really realise it, but there are some long days on the set and it can be a lot of hard work.'
– *Josh Hutcherson*

Josh thought playing alongside Will Ferrell in *Kicking and Screaming* had been a laugh a minute, but nothing could have prepared him for comic genius Robin Williams's off-camera antics when he played Williams's character's son Carl Munro in *RV: Runaway Vacation*. 'Working with Robin is like watching him do stand-up constantly!' Josh later recalled. 'It was so unbelievable to watch him do amazing improvisation. What was fun was getting to improvise along with him because I love to do that, and the fact that I got to do it with Robin Williams still blows my mind.'

Williams plays stressed-out soda company executive Bob Munro, who, having promised his wife Jamie (Cheryl Hines), and kids Carl and Cassie (Joanna 'JoJo' Levesque) that they'd be vacationing in Hawaii, instead has to convince them that a road trip to the Rocky Mountains (where Josh's *Hunger Games* character Peeta Mellark lives in District 12 of the fictional futuristic nation of Panem) will prove more beneficial. But in reality this is so he can save his job – and the family's future – by attending an important business meeting. The Munros may have missed out on Hawaii, and experience a journey fraught with difficulties, but en route they end up re-forging long-forgotten family bonds.

When it was announced Josh had got the part, Michelle was

Opposite: *Josh attends a promotional event for* Firehouse Dog *in 2007.*

hoping it would serve as a boost to Josh's career by exposing him to adult filmgoers drawn by Williams's reputation. She recognised that if acting was to be Josh's lifelong career, he needed to make the transition from 'cute kid' actor to serious professional. 'I think you need to get the audience to see him as an actor and not a child actor,' she said at the time. But whilst she was looking at *RV* as a vital stepping stone to advancing her son's career, Josh was just delighted to be working alongside someone of Williams's stature. '*RV* was so much fun. We had an amazing cast! We all got along so well, and since it was on location, we all did tons of stuff together away from the set and became great friends.'

Josh's 'breakthrough performance' came the following year with *Bridge to Terabithia*. Josh plays preteen Jess Aarons, whose dreams of becoming the fastest runner in school are ruined when he's effortlessly beaten by newcomer Leslie Burke (AnnaSophia Robb). Despite this humiliation, coupled with Leslie being a rich city girl and him being a poor country boy, the two strike up a friendship.

> 'The rewarding side of acting is that I love to travel and I have already travelled a lot and seen a lot of the world.'
> – *Josh Hutcherson*

Together, they create the fantasy realm of Terabithia, a land of ogres, giants, monsters and trolls which they rule together as king and queen. 'I had an interview this one time, and the woman said that the movie was a good conversation starter,' Josh later recalled. 'She kind of wanted to talk to her children about the themes presented in the movie, but she didn't know when or how, so watching it is kind of a good way for parents to talk to their children about some of those things that need to be talked about. I think that is a cool thing about the movie. But at the same time, I do understand some people go into it not expecting that, and they can be a little shocked. They can be like, "Oh crap, my kid just saw that, and now I'm going to have to talk to them about it." But I think that it is a positive thing. I think it is important, and parents will embrace the opportunity.'

Having play-acted discovering being around girls could be fun in

Opposite: Josh celebrates the Japanese release of Bridge to Terabithia *at a stage greeting in Tokyo in 2007.*

Little Manhattan a couple of years previously, Josh now found himself doing it for real on the *Terabithia* set: 'I don't know how we [he and his co-star AnnaSophia] didn't get sick of each other, to be honest with you,' he joked. 'We were together on the set, we were staying in the same room for long periods, and then we were together away from set. [However], we became great friends and I think it shows in the film. We filmed in New Zealand and we took long rides in the country during weekends and hung out a lot. We laughed a lot and got along great. The classroom scenes were fun too. AnnaSophia and I were the only students from America. The rest of the class were New Zealanders.'

'Working with Robin is like watching him do stand-up constantly! It was so unbelievable to watch him do amazing improvisation.'
– Josh Hutcherson

Another girl Josh spent plenty of time with whilst on set was Bailee Madison, who played his on-screen baby sister, May Belle. Indeed, he was so captivated by her that he has often referred to her as the little sister he doesn't have. 'She was amazing in the movie. One day, I was playing and she was filming a scene, and I didn't realise that, and I saw her crying and I was like, "Bailee, what's wrong? Are you okay?" She's like, "Yeah, I'm just getting ready for my scene!"'

'She's the most grown up little person I've ever met. She is the most adorable little kid on the face of the Earth. I love her so much; I honestly don't think I've met anyone like her in my whole life.'

While reading the original book and script for *Bridge to Terabithia*, Josh was initially against being a part of the movie, because he didn't like how the character of Jess treated his younger sister May Belle throughout most of the story. He felt that the character was being so cruel to a little girl who hadn't even done anything wrong, and this really put him off at first. One particular scene called for Josh's character to say to his sister: 'Don't you dare follow us, or I'll tell Alexandra that you still suck your thumb and sleep with Mr Blankie!' This line apparently really upset Bailee because at the time she still

Opposite above: Josh poses with the cast of family-friendly comedy RV *at the film's LA premiere in 2006.* **Opposite below:** *Working with comic legend Robin Williams was a blast.*

Above: *Josh swings between reality and fantasy in 2007's* Bridge to Terabithia.

sucked her thumb and slept with a baby blanket, and thought that Josh was poking fun at her.

Josh (who reportedly had his own security blanket, 'Yellow Blankie', as a kid, which he'd apparently carried around with him everywhere) was only made aware of this whilst doing the commentary for the film's DVD release.

In the accompanying audio commentary that Josh did with AnnaSophia Robb and the film's producer Lauren Levine, Josh expressed his apologies for making the in-school racing scene at the beginning of the film take so long to film. Everyone was trying to work out the timing so AnnaSophia's character Leslie could win the race as scripted, but Josh, being naturally competitive, kept winning race after race, and so it took longer to get the necessary footage.

In the commentary Josh also let it be known that he wasn't all that thrilled with his character's wardrobe. Some scenes called for Jess to walk around with a sweatshirt tied around his waist, which Josh says made him look like he was wearing a kilt. He was also wary about the

Opposite: *Josh poses with his then-girlfriend, model Shanon Wada, at the premiere of* Bridge to Terabithia *in February 2007.*

'If I had to pick just one all-time favourite movie, I guess it would probably be *The Fast and the Furious*. It's a fun movie to watch, and I love cars.'

– *Josh Hutcherson*

crown he had to wear in the final scene. 'I looked like some sort of monk or something,' he groaned.

One of Josh's particular pet hates is travelling long distances either by airplane or car, but a few days after arriving in New Zealand to begin filming *Bridge to Terabithia*, he was called back to Toronto, Canada, to complete some last-minute scenes for *RV*. 'I don't sleep too good on planes, so I get very bored,' he explains. 'I read scripts or watch movies while I'm just sitting there.'

Bridge to Terabithia proved a surprise hit at the box office, and nobody – it seems – was more surprised than Josh: 'Nobody really expected that. Everyone expected it to do okay, but no one expected it to do as well as it did, and that's great. It's a good movie, and it has

'I put myself in the character's role and imagined the character's feelings and that really helped me to do it.'
– Josh Hutcherson

good lessons in it, and it's just nice for that kind of thing to get out there for people to see,' he explained. 'I think it is really cool because throughout the movie, especially Jess, my character, has such a big character arc. He goes from being really reserved, all his emotions inside of him, being so closed off to everything in the world, and then Leslie comes into his life, and it opens everything up.'

Josh's favourite scene in the film also happened to be the most challenging: 'I like the scenes when we fight the creatures in the forest,' he recalled. 'It had a lot of action in it. It was hard because you really had to use your imagination. I have a pretty good imagination and now I have a bit of experience in the business and you learn some things. But it was still a bit challenging. I think it's something that the boys who watch the film will like, with the action in it and everything.'

He added: 'The emotional scenes can [also] be a challenge. There was some sadness but you use your emotions and what helped me was asking myself how I would really feel and act if I were this character.'

What most of Josh's fans remember about *Bridge to Terabithia*, of course, is the crying scene with his on-screen dad, played by *X-Files*

Opposite: Dog-lover Josh poses with his furry co-star at the 2007 premiere of Firehouse Dog.

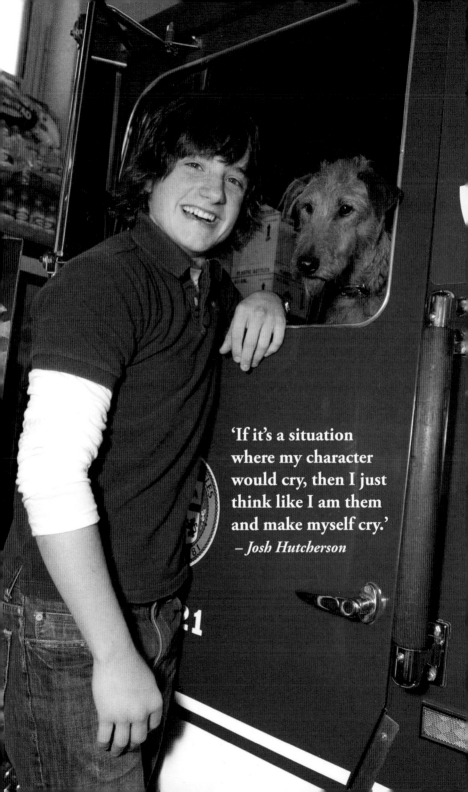

'If it's a situation where my character would cry, then I just think like I am them and make myself cry.'
— *Josh Hutcherson*

Above: *Josh tries to rid himself of a troublesome mutt in* Firehouse Dog.

star Robert Patrick. 'I really did cry in the movie,' Josh says. 'It's what you have to do when you're in character. A lot of people want to know how I make myself cry like that. Well, when I was younger, I would just think of something really sad in my life and cry, but now, what I do is just really get into my character. If it's a situation where my character would cry, then I just think like I am them and make myself cry.'

Director Gabor Csupo was suitably impressed by Josh's ability to shed real tears on demand. 'The scene was amazing, because I think we shot it only twice, and both times, those tears coming out of Joshua's eyes . . . they're real teardrops,' he recalled. 'It's not like we had to physically put them in there with the drop help, or CGI, or anything. These are his real tears. He really melted into this performance so deeply, that even his mom, on the set, was amazed by his performance.'

But of course, while Josh could bask in the plaudits back in Union, he wasn't going to get away without some light-hearted criticism: 'One of my friends said to me, "Dude, maybe sometime, do you want to go rope swinging or something?" And I didn't get it at first, so I was like, "What?" And he said, "You know, go rope swinging," I was like, "Where?" and he was like, "Oh, just any old river valley type of thing," and I was like, "Oh, shut up!"'

In the family film *Firehouse Dog*, Josh plays middle-schooler Shane Fahey, who's struggling with exams and generally suffering from a lack of parental attention and direction owing to his single, fire-fighter dad Marc (Bruce Greenwood) being away from home much of the time. One day, his dad brings home a dog that was rescued from a burning building, which unbeknownst to anyone is actually a movie-star canine named Rexx, who accidentally went astray during a parachuting screen shoot.

'Imagination is an important part of everybody's life. With today's kids, imagination is lost because kids play so many video games.'
– *Josh Hutcherson*

'There actually were four dogs playing Rexx,' Josh told the *Lexington Herald-Leader*. 'It's difficult because they require so much attention and maintenance. [I] had two weeks of bonding with the dogs, but it was more like a business relationship.' Josh was particularly attracted to the script. 'For some reason, it had such a great feel to me. It was unlike any other dog movie, because it had such a cool storyline. It was so different than any other dog movie I had ever seen and ever heard of. That's what really attracted me to it – that it was so unique.'

Another reason, of course, could be that it gave him the chance to work with dogs every single day on set. But this wasn't without its requisite problems, as he explained: 'The problem was that my dog, Diesel, got jealous. I was spending so much time on set with the other dogs that he was like, "Hey man, what's up? What's going on?"

'Diesel [a two-year-old Boxer] is nuts, he's crazy,' he chuckled. 'He loves to go to the dog park, but if you throw a ball, he won't chase the ball. He'll chase whatever dog is chasing the ball.'

THE KID IS ALL RIGHT

'I am very critical of myself on screen. I can never just sit back and enjoy the movie. I find myself critiquing myself a lot.'
– *Josh Hutcherson*

Another parallel between Josh and Jennifer's careers is that Josh had to learn how to chop wood for *Firehouse Dog*. But whereas Jennifer was required to learn how to chop firewood for *Winter's Bone*, Josh had to take lessons in using an axe for a scene in which he is trapped in a house fire. 'I had to really work hard to chop away at the door.' he said. 'It was a tough scene to do because of the smoke. I actually got a bit congested and coughed for a while when that scene was finished.'

The *Lexington Herald-Leader* caught up with Josh shortly after he finished filming, and it appears that whilst there aren't many downsides to making movies, one would most definitely be the unavailability of his favourite chilli (Skyline Chilli) in Hollywood.

With *Firehouse Dog* now added to his rapidly growing film résumé, Josh didn't have much free time. But as soon as the cameras had finished rolling, he and Michelle would fly back to Union. When he wasn't catching up on his schooling, he could more often than not be found riding his motorised scooter up and down Tender Court, going to the Paul Brown Stadium to cheer on his favourite football team, the Cincinnati Bengals, or hanging out with friends at the Florence Shopping Mall, 'chowing down' on his favourite chilli. 'When I'm not filming movies I love being home and getting to do normal kid things with my friends,' he said. 'It's kind of weird to think about

Opposite: Sundance kid: Josh poses for his official portrait during the twenty-ninth year of the legendary film festival in 2010.

Above: *Josh at the 2008 premiere of* Journey to the Centre of the Earth.

'When I'm not filming movies I love being at home and getting to do normal kid things with my friends.'
– *Josh Hutcherson*

it, [but] it's like, "Whoa, I never thought I'd get this far."'

2008 brought Josh another action-packed role in Eric Brevig's 3-D remake of the 1959 film adaptation of Jules Verne's classic tale *Journey to the Centre of the Earth*, playing Sean Anderson, the nephew of Brendan Fraser's character, Professor Trevor Anderson.

Sean is spending some 'quality time' with his uncle while his mother Elizabeth (Jane Wheeler) prepares for their move to Canada. But the professor has come upon a book containing references to the last journey of his brother Max, and having decided to follow his brother's trail, he and Sean travel to Iceland, where they encounter local guide Hannah Ásgeirsson (Anita Briem).

Whilst climbing a mountain the three get caught up in a thunderstorm and seek shelter within a cave. However, when a lightning bolt collapses the cave's entrance, the trio are forced to head into the cave in search of an exit, and in turn discover a lost world within the centre of the earth. 'It has a lot of action and excitement in it,' Josh says. 'We travel down to the earth's core and have to escape from flowing lava. It's really good. It's a cliff-hanger kind of story.'

Above: *Brendan Fraser and Anita Briem help Josh to search for his missing father in big-budget blockbuster,* Journey to the Centre of the Earth.

While Josh has gone on record saying making *Journey to the Centre of the Earth* was the most physically gruelling experience of his acting career to date, he says he enjoyed all the additional stunt work that they got to do.

Though *The Hunger Games* will be compared with *Twilight,* Josh has already been bloodied in that respect with *Cirque du Freak: The Vampire's Assistant,* which Universal had hoped would turn into a '*Twilight* for boys'. Unfortunately, the film wasn't particularly well-received and grossed just $34 million worldwide.

In the film Josh plays the reckless Steve, who cajoles his best friend – straight-A student Darren (Chris Massoglia), into accompanying him to a travelling circus, whose ringmaster (John C. Reilly) is a vampire. 'My character Steve is a "vampaneze", which is basically an evil vampire,' Josh told *J-14*. 'And the difference between the vampires and vampaneze is that the vampires live by a certain code – they can't kill, they can't do certain things, and they only drink blood to survive. My character is the reckless type and that was really fun to play. It's definitely different than anything I've played before because I haven't ever really got the chance to play the bad guy kind of role.'

Above: *No more Mr Nice Guy: Josh gets in touch with his dark side in 2009's* The Vampire's Assistant.

'I'm a big fan of the older vampire movies like *The Lost Boys* and *Interview with the Vampire*,' Josh said in an interview with *Seventeen* magazine. 'But I also like *Twilight* a lot. I'm excited to see *New Moon*; the new trailer looks really cool. It's cool to play a vampire. Vampires can do whatever they want whenever they want, like fly around all the time. Plus, girls love vampires. Maybe they don't want to admit it, but they do, which is a plus.'

> **'It's cool to play a vampire. Vampires can do whatever they want whenever they want.'**
> **– Josh Hutcherson**

Despite his hectic filming schedule, Josh still found time for the opposite sex. His first 'serious' girlfriend was aspiring actress and occasional model Shannon Wada. But while he was happy to be photographed with Shannon at film premieres and other celebrity occasions, he understandably preferred to keep his personal life exactly that. However, on his official website he said that he and Shannon met through one of his friends, and not on a film set as gossips were hinting.

Opposite: *Josh flashes a signature smile at the 2009 Teen Choice Awards in LA.*

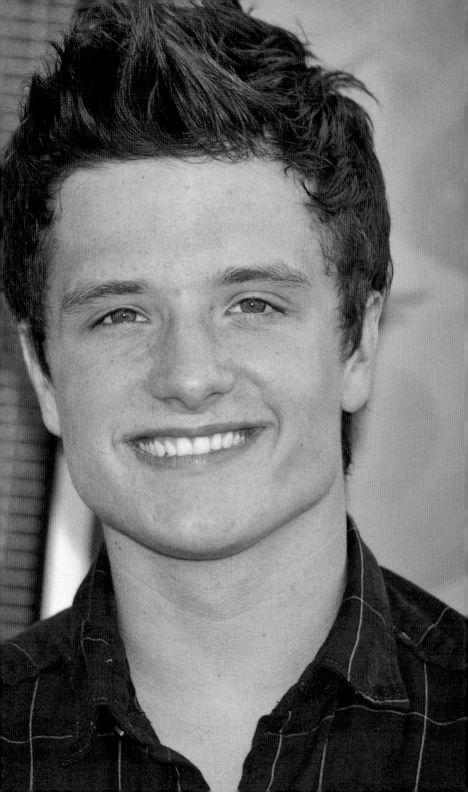

Above: Josh poses with his on-screen family at the 2010 premiere of The Kids Are All Right.

'I like both athletic girls and girlie girls,' he says. 'It depends on their personality. I like girls who can go out and play sports with me and throw the football around, but you don't want a girl who's too much tougher than you.'

In 2010 Josh landed the role of Laser in the critically acclaimed film *The Kids Are All Right*, in which Annette Bening and Julianne Moore play Nic and Jules, who are in a long-term, loving – but by no means perfect – lesbian relationship. Jules is Laser's biological mother, whilst Nic has a daughter called Joni (Mia Wasikowska).

Joni and Laser are actually half-siblings as their mothers both received sperm from the same unknown donor, and each has a different reaction when the donor – who is technically their father – enters their lives. '[The writers] Lisa [Cholodenko, who also directs

Opposite: When you're smiling: Josh has every reason to grin as he picks up the 2010 Breakthrough of the Year award for The Kids Are All Right.

'If a girl shows any interest, I'm like, "Yes! I love you, you're amazing!"'
– *Josh Hutcherson*

Above: *The kid's all grown up: Josh's performance as Laser in* The Kids Are All Right *signalled his graduation from child star to serious actor.*

the film] and Stuart [Blumberg] did a great job of capturing these characters and the essence of who they were. They worked on it for almost five years. For me I just played the part that was on the page,' Josh said. 'Laser is a teen who's trying to figure out who he is and how he fits into the world, and I know I identified with that. I'm pretty sure that most teenagers out there – and adults who have ever been teenagers – can identify with that as well.'

He continued: 'Ever since I first started acting I've wanted to have a long career. This is just a step in the direction of becoming more of an adult actor. The story was so real and it encapsulated the family and depicted it in a way that has never been done before, and it definitely is a genre and a type of movie I haven't been part of before, and I loved it. As an actor I feel like a lot of times your job is to portray real life or the complete opposite, a fantastical world. I've done a lot of fantastical crazy stuff that doesn't exist, so to break it down into something that was so real and genuine like this was really fun and different.'

Because of the success of *Journey to the Centre of the Earth*, Josh was invited to reprise the role of Sean Anderson for *Journey 2: The Mysterious Island*, in which he stars opposite Michael Caine and *High School Musical* star Vanessa Hudgens. In the film, Josh's character partners with his mother's boyfriend Hank (Dwayne 'The Rock' Johnson) on a mission to find his grandfather (Caine), who is stranded on the legendary island of the title.

Josh was rumoured to be Sony's preferred choice to play Peter Parker in the new *Spider-Man* film before losing out to surprise selection Andrew

Above: *Josh poses with his* Journey 2: The Mysterious Island *co-star Vanessa Hudgens.*

Garfield, and another false start seems to be the still-to-be released remake of the 1984 Patrick Swayze film *Red Dawn*, in which he coincidentally plays alongside Chris Hemsworth, the older brother of his future *Hunger Games* co-star, Liam.

Though the film has been completed, it has apparently been put on indefinite hold owing to MGM's rumoured financial troubles. One film that is set for release in 2012, however, is *Carmel*, in which Josh plays a teenager who gets himself involved with a set of art forgers in Carmel, California.

'[The past year has] been crazy,' Josh told MTV. 'I shot *Journey 2: The Mysterious Island* the end of last year and the beginning of this year, then I went into a little short film I shot in Cuba with Benicio Del Toro called *7 dias en La Habana* [*Seven Days in Havana*], which was really fun, and then this summer the whole time I spent shooting

'The fans mean the world to me. Without the fans, I wouldn't have a job.'
– *Josh Hutcherson*

The Hunger Games, which was an amazing experience. Very exciting, and I can't wait for that to come out.'

Neither, of course, can his ever-growing legion of adoring fans. 'They [the fans] mean the world to me. Without the fans, I wouldn't have a job. When people hire you for a movie, they want to hire you because you're going to bring an audience to their film. If I didn't have people out there who enjoyed watching me as an actor, I wouldn't get hired. Nobody would want to see the movie!'

Rumours soon began flying around Hollywood that Josh and Vanessa were an item, but when *Seventeen* magazine subsequently pressed him for confirmation that the two were seeing each other, Josh played it down: 'Oh, boy. I don't know if "dating" is the right word,' he said cagily. 'She's awesome. We love being together. When I first met her, we just really hit it off. We could be goofy and silly and not worry about anything except having fun. I adore her.'

'As an actor I feel like your job is to portray real life or the complete opposite, a fantastical world.'
– *Josh Hutcherson*

He then went on to say what traits Vanessa – or any other potential girlfriend – would need: 'I like girls I can have deep conversations with. The meaning of life and existence — you can go on forever about that stuff. When girls play the ditzy-dumb thing, I'm like, "Oh, God, please stop."'

Josh says his life is so normal that he still gets grounded by his parents, which must come as a bind seeing as he's recently gained his driving license. His passion for fast cars is well-known, but even he must have been pinching himself when he was invited to serve as the Grand Marshal at the Indy Racing League Indy-Car Series Meijer Indy 300 at the Kentucky Speedway in August 2011 – one of the many perks of his success. 'I love what I do, and I can't imagine ever wanting to do anything else, except maybe direct. So, as long as I am able to, I want to keep acting. Anything that comes my way, I'm open to it. If it's a good script and everything's right, I'll pursue it.'

Opposite: *Josh looks sharp at GQ's Men of the Year Awards 2011.*

GALE HAWTHORNE
THE BOY WITH THE SNARES

Casting for the most anticipated cinematic love triangle since *Twilight* trio Edward, Bella and Jacob traded love bites was completed when Lionsgate officially announced that Aussie heartthrob Liam Hemsworth would play Gale Hawthorne in *The Hunger Games*.

Josh, of course, was already well-known in Hollywood and was also long-anticipated to snag one of the lead roles in the film, whereas Liam – despite having been placed well ahead of Josh on *InStyle's* 'Twenty Most Stylish Men of 2011' list – had just one major role to his name and was a comparative unknown in Tinseltown. And it's fair to say that while Jennifer and Josh landing the roles of Katniss and Peeta caught the trilogy's ever-burgeoning fan-base by surprise, Liam being cast as Gale had them tweeting long into the night.

Like Josh, 21-year-old Liam, whose older brother Chris pipped him for the lead role in actor-turned director Kenneth Branagh's 2011 superhero film *Thor*, knew immediately which part he wanted to play from his first reading of the *Hunger Games* script. 'It was always for Gale,' he told *Vanity Fair*. 'I read the script, and Gale definitely felt more right than Peeta. What I thought was really interesting was – and it's one of the hardest things to think about – one of your best friends, or someone in your family, basically going off to war. And that's kind of what happens to Gale in the first book. As much as he's against the government and wants to stand up to them, he really is helpless. He can't do anything about it . . . I just thought it was such a gut-wrenching kind of thought.'

Opposite: Leading Man: 2010 saw Liam go from relative unknown to Hollywood heartthrob.

FOLLOWING IN FAMILY FOOTSTEPS

'Acting is always hard work, but I enjoy it.
When I was in Georgia, I would prefer to be working
than having a day off. I enjoyed being on set. I love working
with people, other actors. That's why I do it.'
– *Liam Hemsworth*

L iam Hemsworth was born on 13 January 1990 in Melbourne, Australia, and spent the first thirteen years of his life growing up in Victoria's state capital before the family upped sticks and relocated to the rather more sedate surroundings of Phillip Island; a thirty-nine-square-mile atoll which lays within the shallow waters of Westernport Bay, some eighty-seven miles further along the coast.

Moving from a sprawling metropolis like Melbourne to a tiny island with a population of just 10,000 – where, if Liam is to be believed, life is so laidback that there is no need for shopping malls or traffic lights – would have come as something of a culture shock had it not been for his new home having sixty miles of meandering coastline, where he and his brothers Luke and Chris spent much of their free time swimming and surfing.

Given that he was now living on an island connected to the mainland by a solitary concrete bridge, it is not all that surprising that 'catching the waves' quickly became his *raison d'être*. 'I've always loved surfing,' he revealed. 'When I was at school that was pretty much all that mattered in my life. Most of my friends surfed so we would go before school, after school, literally whenever we could.

'There's always a swell at Phillip Island, which is why I love it there. The thing with LA is, it's good when it's on, but a lot of the time

Opposite: *Attending a dinner for Australia's Foxtel TV
company before his big break, Liam already looks like a star.*

there's not too much swell.' And so when he was asked to name a male non-actor whom he admires, Liam's answer didn't come as much of a surprise to anyone who knows him. Of course, he picked American surfer Kelly Slater, the eleven-time ASP champion. 'That's definitely something to admire,' he enthused.

Of course, with his blonde hair, striking looks, and 'ripped bod' from all the surfing and swimming he was doing, Liam had all the local girls mooning over him. 'He was the new boy at school and all the girls liked him,' former high-school classmate and ex-girlfriend Laura Griffin recalled for *Woman's Day* magazine. 'He was popular, a bit of a joker and he made me laugh. We became inseparable. He tried to teach me to surf, we watched movies, and went shopping. Liam became more than a boyfriend, he was my best friend.'

'I've always loved surfing. When I was at school that was pretty much all that mattered in my life.'
– Liam Hemsworth

Laura, who's now twenty-two, would also have us believe that their relationship continued long after Liam moved to Los Angeles to further his acting career, and that when she saw her actor boyfriend of five years passionately kissing the world's most famous teenager, Miley Cyrus, in *The Last Song*, she'd believed he was only doing his job. But, of course, Liam wasn't faking, and shortly after completing the film, he jetted back to Phillip Island to break up with Laura, so that he'd be free to date Miley. 'We became inseparable [and] there's no other reason why we would have broken up,' she told the magazine.

There's no denying Liam has come a long way both geographically and career-wise in the three years since he played the paraplegic Josh Taylor in long-running Aussie soap opera *Neighbours* (which proved a springboard for his fellow actor Guy Pearce – who recently played King Edward VIII in the Oscar-winning 2010 film *The King's Speech* – as well as pop princesses Natalie Imbruglia and Kylie Minogue).

Playing the role of a wheelchair-bound paraplegic was a rather demanding one for Liam, as he had to master getting around in a wheelchair whilst making it look authentic. And of course, things didn't always go according to plan: '[I] just turned up on set, sat in a

Above: *All in the family: Chris and Liam Hemsworth with their parents in 2006.*

wheelchair. The producer came up to me one day and said, "We have to cut around that entire scene because your leg was moving.'"

His on-screen relationship with Bridget (Eloise Mignon), who'd been left paralysed down one side of her body following a car crash, touched the collective heart of viewers, and though he'd actually made a one-off appearance in *Neighbours'* one-time arch-rival for the Aussie soap crown, *Home and Away*, as he went on to make twenty-five appearances in *Neighbours*, the show's fans obviously forgave him for his transgression.

Unlike his older brothers, Liam grew up with no real acting aspirations, and only began to seriously consider following in their footsteps in the final year of high school. 'I saw my brother doing it and thought I could do it better,' he subsequently joked.

Though he hired an agent, he was working regular nine-to-five jobs, serving as an usher of sorts during the island's annual 'Penguin

Parade' (Phillip Island is home to the Little – or 'Fairy' – Penguin), as well as laying floors for a local construction company – all of which he was able to give up on landing the part of Damo in the Logie Award-winning drama series *McLeod's Daughters* in 2007. 'I was laying floors for six months and I can tell you acting is definitely better,' he subsequently told Melbourne's *Herald Sun*. 'It makes me really appreciate what I have got at the moment.'

It was his performance in *Neighbours* which undoubtedly led to him being offered the role of guitar-playing Marcus in successful children's television series *The Elephant Princess*. Liam's final appearances on Australian TV, however, came in the rather more adult-orientated drama series *Satisfaction*, which was set in a brothel and explored the seedy world of prostitution. 'I played a sixteen-year-old who hires a prostitute,' he later said of the part. 'I was butt-naked in front of fifty people, which is totally comfortable.'

Liam's first film role came in the 2009 low-budget British horror flick *Triangle*, in which he plays Victor, one of the hapless passengers who seek refuge on a mysterious ship when their yacht flounders in bad weather out on the Atlantic Ocean. This was followed with another bit part in Egyptian-born director Alex Proyas's *Knowing*, a sci-fi mystery shot in Australia, which tells about an MIT teacher (Nicolas Cage) who opens a time capsule that has been dug up at his son's elementary school and believes he's discovered a pattern that predicts fatal disasters.

'I think I had two or three lines, [but it] was really cool because I got to meet Alex Proyas and work with him for two days,' Liam said. 'But it was more the fact that the two days I was there, the camera was on Nicolas Cage most of the time and I could just sit there and watch him, which was really, really cool. He [Cage] is just so professional in what he does. You know, he won't really talk to anyone between takes; he'll talk to the director, but he keeps very much to himself. He's just amazing; you can tell when he's looking at you that he's got so much going on in his head. There's so much going on in his eyes.'

No sooner had Liam finished the film, however, than – following older brother Chris's example – he boarded a Qantas flight bound

Opposite: Brotherly love: Liam and Chris attend the Australians in Film Breakthrough Awards, where Chris picked up a boomerang for his hammer-swinging role in Thor.

'Maybe I wouldn't have become an actor if my older brothers weren't actors, but now that I'm here, I really enjoy it and it's what I feel most comfortable doing.'
– *Liam Hemsworth*

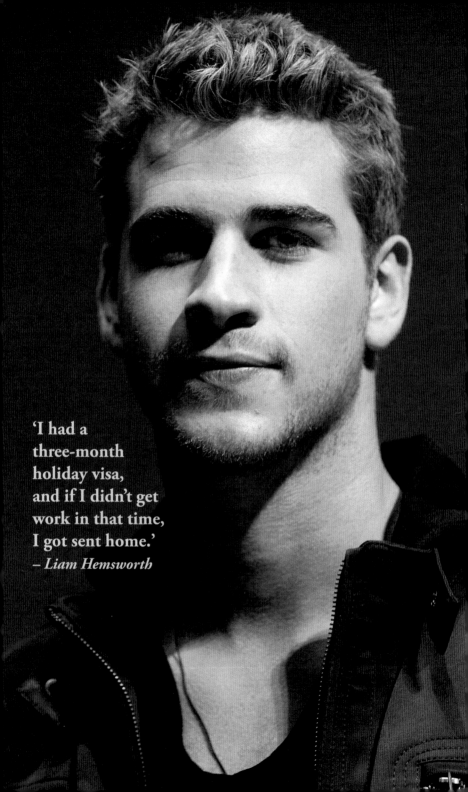

'I had a
three-month
holiday visa,
and if I didn't get
work in that time,
I got sent home.'
– *Liam Hemsworth*

for Los Angeles in order to further his acting career. 'I think when I started acting, the whole time I was working towards one day coming to America. Hollywood, in particular, is seen to be the centre of this industry, and I was just waiting for the right time to come,' he said. 'I'd gotten flown over for *Thor*, so that was kind of the right time for me. And it definitely feels like I'm doing the right thing, and in the right spot.'

Though Liam's bank balance is looking rather healthy these days, at the time he didn't have much in the way of savings and – albeit temporarily – joined his brother, Chris, in living with Chris's agent William Ward while trying out for parts. 'I had a three-month holiday visa, and if I didn't get work in that time, I got sent home. I was nineteen at the time. It's a big deal. I was really scared. The biggest thing in my mind was not succeeding. That would have been embarrassing.'

Needless to say, with Chris's star steadily rising, he and Liam were soon able to get an apartment of their own, but any thoughts of reliving their youth – going surfing together off Malibu, or throwing parties – were soon dashed as, due to their work commitments, they were never in the apartment at the same time.

Liam took to Los Angeles like the proverbial Aussie to a barbecue, but, like his future *Hunger Games* co-star Jennifer, he found New York equally invigorating: 'I love New York. It just reminds me of so many movies . . . I look up at buildings, and feel like Godzilla should be climbing up them or something. I tried to get out and see it a bit – I went out to a sushi place and they served me sushi on an oar!'

Of course, aside from finding work and a place of his own, one of the first things Liam had to tend to after arriving in Los Angeles was his American accent. It wasn't that Australian actors couldn't get work in Hollywood – Hugh Jackman's success is testament to the contrary. Indeed, there is a thriving Australian ex-pat community in LA, but being able to slip into the American vernacular at will would help his chances considerably. 'It's not easy,' he admitted. 'I did a film [*Triangle*] just before I came to America, in an American accent. So I've worked with an accent coach before, and I worked with an accent coach on this as well. I do a lot of work with it. And we grew up with

Opposite: Liam promotes Australia's Foxtel Television network in Sydney in 2009.

more than half of our television being American TV, and we watch a lot of the same movies that you guys do. It definitely takes work, but I've done it my whole life. You have times when things slip for whatever reason, but I just try not to think about those times.'

2009 saw Liam being chosen out of a string of hopefuls for Sylvester Stallone's *The Expendables*, in which the *Rocky* and *Rambo* star would also appear alongside Jason Statham, Bruce Willis, Mickey Rourke, and Jet Li. However, before he could start practicing his 'action moves', his character was written out of the script. According to Chris – who would subsequently land the part of the fantasy warrior – it was within a day or two of learning that he wouldn't be appearing in *The Expendables* that Kenneth Branagh called to ask Liam to test for the lead role in his film, *Thor*.

> **'I love New York. It just reminds me of so many movies . . . I look up at buildings, and feel like Godzilla should be climbing up them or something.'**
> *– Liam Hemsworth*

'I was at my friend's house and I got a phone call from my Australian agent, who had sent my tape in a few days before,' Liam recalled. 'He said, "Stallone is going to call you in a few days," and I went back into my buddy's house and said, "Rocky's gonna give me a call, no big deal." He [Stallone] called a few days later and it was weird to be speaking to him on the phone in my house while I am looking at his DVDs of *Rocky* and *Rambo* on the shelf.

'I was about to go over for that when the script was completely rewritten and six characters got cut. Mine was one of them. That was a big kick in the guts.'

Though doubly disappointed over his *Expendables* character being deemed surplus to requirements even before the shooting started, as well as missing out on playing the comic-book superhero, Liam was happy that the *Thor* role remained in the family. And he was insistent that, while there was competition between him and his brothers for acting parts, it was never anything other than friendly: 'I punched him in the head. No [seriously], I'm happier for him to get it than someone else. My brother's playing Thor. That's cool as shit. There is [competition], but not in a bad way. We are brothers and we are always competitive.'

Above: *Attending the* Thor *premiere in May 2011, Liam and Chris Hemsworth have taken Tinseltown by storm.*

He added: 'I'm the youngest so I always looked up to [Chris and Luke], and I was always influenced by what they were doing. Maybe I wouldn't have become an actor if my older brothers weren't actors, but now that I'm here, I really enjoy it and it's what I feel most comfortable doing. We've always been super-competitive. We push each other to do better, but at the end of the day we're all really close and really happy for each other to succeed.'

This good-natured sibling rivalry was backed up by big brother Chris: 'The three of us have always been really close, and it's not a spiteful, competitive kind of thing. We're always kind of asking each other, "How did we get in this position?" To be involved in any of this stuff is kind of a trip for us.'

FIRST GIG, THE LAST SONG

'Hollywood's been nothing but fantastic to me.
Hollywood's amazing; it's opened a lot of doors.'
– *Liam Hemsworth*

Liam's disappointment would thankfully prove to be short-lived, as the same week he lost the *Thor* role to Chris, Disney called to say he'd landed the part of Will Blakelee in their forthcoming film, *The Last Song*, which was based on the Nicholas Sparks novel of the same name. 'Within one week – it was probably the biggest week of our lives – I booked *The Last Song*, Chris booked *Thor* and then he booked *Red Dawn*,' Liam recalled for the *Herald Sun*. 'That was three studio films between us, so it was a really, really happy week for us. It has been an amazing couple of years.'

In *The Last Song*, an inspiring coming-of-age story about first love, Liam plays the love interest of co-star Miley Cyrus's character Ronnie. Having lived with their mother following their parents' divorce, Ronnie and her younger brother, Jonah (Bobby Coleman), are sent to live with their father (Greg Kinnear) in a remote coastal town. Ronnie has a troubled relationship with her father and makes no secret of the resentment she feels towards him. But after meeting handsome local Will Blakelee, she starts rediscovering her love for music – a passion she shares with her father.

'I knew who she [Miley] was, but I didn't know how big she was around the world really,' Liam said of his co-star. 'But that was a good thing. It meant that it was a girl that I was meeting rather than a star and

Opposite: Liam acts cool as he becomes Hollywood hot property.

'It's a really beautiful story. It's love and romance; reconnecting with family.'

– Liam Hemsworth

it was great. From the first time I met her she was so kind and so easy and really nice. Her music is awesome. She's incredibly talented. I'd never heard her before meeting her and I was pleasantly surprised. I don't know how she does what she does. She works literally every day, recording on weekends, and filming during the week – her work ethic is incredible.'

Liam said that he and Miley got along from day one on the set. 'For some people it can be an effort to find that chemistry but we just worked really well

Above: Liam poses with writer Nicholas Sparks at the 2010 premiere of The Last Song.

together,' he told *Dolly* magazine. 'It is a funny thing; I have known people who hate each other in real life but have amazing chemistry on screen. We don't hate each other in life. We get along really well so it just worked on screen – and we get along really well together in real life too.'

Though Liam was unfamiliar with the storyline of *The Last Song*, he was familiar with the book's author Nicholas Sparks's other works. 'I'd seen *The Notebook* before and thought that was a really great story, and [when] I got this script and thought it was a great story, too; I think Nicholas Sparks, he's got the power to affect people in some way or another. His stories incorporate so many different emotions, and have really good messages about family and love and friendship. I

Opposite: Liam and co-star girlfriend Miley Cyrus are all smiles at The Last Song's *premiere.*

think that's why they do so well. I felt the same way about this story; it's about a girl growing up and getting to know her father, and falling in love and dealing with responsibilities that come with that. And dealing with death, also.

'The most difficult stuff for me is emotional stuff, because you want it to all look real obviously,' he continued. 'For me that's the hardest – bringing up that emotion. It's a really hard to talk about anything very personal and emotional to a girl. I think that was the thing about Will and Ronnie and why they have a deep relationship; he realised that he could tell this girl anything at all.'

While empathising with the storyline, however, Liam insists he's nothing like Will Blakelee in real life. 'I'm nothing like my character in the film, not at all, to be honest,' Liam told *Teen Vogue*. 'He's very persistent when Miley's character gives him the brush off. If I was to get turned down by a girl, I'd just give up and say, "Oh well." I don't have any of that kind of motivation to keep going. I would just be embarrassed and would try to never think about it again if I was to get turned down. I would find it humiliating.'

> **'I read the script and then I got called back and read with Miley and got the part; it was exciting.'**
> **– Liam Hemsworth**

Liam arrived on set that first day knowing that *The Last Song* could either make or break his career, and so being informed by director Julie Anne Robinson that a kiss had been written into one of that day's scenes would surely have done nothing to calm his already fraying nerves. 'It's funny, because I didn't actually know there was going to be a kiss in that scene; it wasn't in the script,' he later recalled. 'In the script it just said we were running through the water, having fun and splashing . . . about halfway through the screen, Julie Anne yelled out, "Kiss!" And we kissed. It was kind of a good way to do it, because neither of us had time to get nervous about having a first kiss in front of a hundred people. It was good, we just got right into it, and then you've got the first kiss out of the way and you're fine!'

Despite having the kiss scene unexpectedly thrown his way on

Opposite: I Love New York: Liam poses on the streets of the Big Apple in 2010.

'I've always been pretty energetic, I grew up surfing and I do a lot of boxing and kickboxing and stuff.'
— *Liam Hemsworth*

Above: *Liam and proud mum Leonie at the Melbourne premiere of* The Last Song *in 2010.*

the first day, Liam thoroughly enjoyed working with Julie Anne. 'She [Robinson] was amazing; she's such a kind person and always makes you feel really comfortable in a scene. It's just calm on set, which is great. You can relax and do your thing and she's very easygoing. She collaborates and often asked me, "What do you want to do in this scene and what do you feel about the scene?" It's great to be able to talk to a director like that and share ideas.'

Liam's first scene was slightly less intimidating, as instead of puckering up to Miley he only had to strip down to his waist: 'I knew I was going to [have to] get my top off a few times so I thought I'd make it pay,' he told the *Daily Telegraph*. 'But it was a character decision. He's a star volleyball player and he's athletic. I'm not going to have a six-pack for a film unless I have to. I'm going to stay true to the role. I mean, if I'm playing someone who is overweight . . .

'I got the role probably four weeks before we started shooting and I started training immediately. I've always been pretty energetic, I grew up surfing and I do a lot of boxing and kickboxing and stuff so I was already pretty fit. But [leading up to *The Last Song*] I had a personal trainer six days a week.'

Opposite: *Liam answers viewer's questions about* The Last Song *on Canadian music video channel MuchMusic in March 2010.*

Flexing his 'pecs' in preparation for going in front of the camera was one thing, but little could he have imagined that he'd also be called upon to loosen his vocal chords. 'That wasn't even in the script,' Liam said about his singing in the film. 'I just started singing along and then they said, "Do more," and I said, "Oh, no," and they said, "But that was so funny." I was laughing the whole way through that scene because I was like, "This is going to ruin my career."'

Perhaps not surprisingly, given that *The Last Song* was his first major screen role, Liam found the whole experience overwhelming: 'At the start of this year, I flew to LA to do a screen test for a film that my brother ended up getting. There are a billion people there trying to do what we do. The first day, I walked out, and one end of the beach was blocked off for fans – screaming kids. I'd never seen that before. It was quite amazing.'

> **'We're both really proud of the work we did in that film and, yeah, we are great friends.'**
>
> *– Liam Hemsworth*

He was understandably proud of the finished film: 'I think it's great. I'm really proud of it,' he said. 'I'll have to watch it again though, because I spent the whole time basically just critiquing myself. I had a lot of fun filming it.'

As with Jennifer and Nicholas Hoult, and Josh and Vanessa Hudgens, Liam's on-screen romance with Miley developed into something away from the cameras. However, as their romance was in its infancy, both he and Miley were naturally keen to play things down. Indeed, Liam went so far as to deny outright that they were an item when the glossies starting prying into his personal life. Though he'd been something of a celebrity back in Australia, it was nothing compared to what he could expect in Hollywood. 'We are great friends,' he insisted. 'We shot a film together for three months and we are both really proud of the work we did in that film and, yeah, we are great friends.

'Working with Miley was a lot easier than I thought it was going to be. From the first time we read, it was like I had known her before.'

Opposite: *Liam returns to Australia to host Nickelodeon's Kids' Choice Awards in 2010.*

And when Miley was called upon to explain their relationship, she proved equally vague: 'It sucks when your personal life becomes public . . . So I'm finding ways to make my personal and private life more of my life – which is one of the reasons why I deleted my Twitter,' she told *Seventeen* magazine. 'We've decided that any type of relationship that we have, we will always just keep it very DL [Down-Low]. First and foremost, we are best friends, so that's what I tell people all the time.'

Their repeated denials, however, were fooling no one – especially not the glossy gossip columnists. And once the news became official, MTV caught up with Miley and asked her how she'd nabbed her Aussie hunk. '[Our first kiss] was on the first day of filming in the movie,' she said. 'We have this scene where we frolic in the water. I frolic very well apparently . . . and after that I got to keep him.

'I've never gotten along with someone so well,' she cooed. 'I was a little anxious about making this movie; I wanted everything to be perfect. To go on set and feel insecure was a totally new element for me. But he felt the same way. He admitted his insecurities, and it was really nice to have someone who understands me for once.'

Above: Liam and Miley share their first kiss – on screen – whilst filming The Last Song *in 2010.* ***Opposite:*** *Liam plays popular and good-looking Will Blakelee in the same movie.*

'From the first time I met her she was so kind and so easy and really nice. Her music is awesome. She's incredibly talented. I'd never heard her sing before meeting her and I was pleasantly surprised.'
– *Liam Hemsworth*

Another factor in Miley's falling for Liam was what she described as his 'old-school chivalry': '[When] I met him he opened the door for me, and I was like, "I have been in LA for three years, and I don't think any guy has actually opened the door for me. It wasn't that he wanted the job. That's just who he is. I was like, "Wow, that is super-impressive." I actually turned to the director and said, "He's got the job. He's hot and he opened the door. Excellent."'

Miley subsequently told the *Daily Telegraph*: 'We balance each other. I make him look good. He makes me look good. I think that's why the on-screen chemistry was so amazing, because we really do have feelings for each other. The last thing I was expecting to do was fall in love. But I guess God was like, "Girl, here is this amazing guy." Liam has become my best friend in the whole wide world. I love him.'

And Liam was finally equally forthcoming in an interview with *clevvertv.com*. After raving about how amazing Miley was, being able to 'sing, dance, and act', he confirmed the rumours by saying: 'I get nervous talking about my private life, but it's hard to deny . . . so many photos.'

While Miley had been bowled over by Liam's gentlemanly charm and manners, Liam revealed what it was about Miley that floated his boat: 'There is this place in Nashville [where Miley was born] called Steak and Shake, which is pretty much the best food, ever. That is our secret, sexy place to go. When I look over at her when she's biting into a steak sandwich and there is some steak sauce dripping down her chin, there is nothing sexier than that.'

On a more serious note, however, he added: 'The main thing is that we know how we feel. We know what's going on. It can get complicated bringing the rest of the world into it.'

He also went on to explain that honesty is the most important part of his relationship: 'I like to put things on the table. I like when other people do that as well – you don't really get anywhere if you keep it all bottled up. You need to talk about it.'

Miley had only recently split from aspiring actor/musician Justin Gaston when she arrived on set to begin filming *The Last Song*, so the last thing she would have been expecting was to fall for her co-star. 'I came to Tybee Island crying harder than I had ever cried in

Opposite: Miley and Liam's Last Song *love story continues off-screen as the couple are seen out and about in LA in June 2010.*

my life, and I left with the biggest smile on my face,' she told *Teen Vogue* during an interview with her and Liam in Miley's hotel suite. But dating a strapping six-foot-three Aussie hunk did present certain problems for the diminutive five-foot-four singer. 'He's really tall,' she said. 'I thought, either I'm going to have to be in heels or standing on something for this entire movie!'

Hollywood loves a true-life romance almost as much as it does the tearjerkers it puts up on the big screen, and Liam and Miley found themselves the glossy columnists' latest darlings. But whilst Miley had learnt to live her life in the camera lens, Liam found it rather more frustrating: 'I get frustrated a lot but the best thing to do is just smile and go on your way,' he said. 'If you do anything else you just end up looking stupid anyway. Whatever you do, you have to think about – so I definitely leave the house with pants on. Usually.'

> **'I make him look good. He makes me look good. I think that's why the on-screen chemistry was so amazing, because we really do have feelings for each other.'** – *Miley Cyrus*

While Liam and Miley strived to keep their romance private, they couldn't keep themselves hidden away 24/7, and were 'papped' coming out of film premieres, going into restaurants or taking strolls along Hollywood Boulevard. And now that their romance was out in the open, Liam joked with reporters about putting signed pictures of himself up on Miley's bedroom wall, and saying how Miley did a lot of dancing around the house as part of her daily workout.

It seemed as though Liam and Miley's relationship had definitely stepped up a gear when Miley saw the New Year in with Liam and his family on Phillip Island. 'SUPERSTAR teen Miley Cyrus has seemingly kicked off the new year on Phillip Island with her boyfriend, rising Aussie star Liam Hemsworth,' was how the *Herald Sun* reported the sighting, before going on to reveal that Miley was believed to have slipped into Melbourne from London on New Year's Eve after completing her world tour.

Opposite: Liam accepts Young Hollywood's Breakthrough of the Year Award for 2010.

The Melbourne paper hinted that Liam – who'd already met Miley's mom Cindy and her multi-platinum-selling country-and-western star dad, Billy Ray – had invited Miley so that she could meet his mum and dad, Leonie and Craig, and his brother Luke, who also still lived on the island. 'Yeah, they loved her,' Liam beamed. 'It was really cool to show Miley where I'm from and how I grew up. And it's a completely different world to where she's from.'

Miley, however, subsequently said of her time on Phillip Island: 'I went to Australia to visit him and his family and I was like, "Ohmigosh, this looks like Nashville." There were like cows everywhere. I am like, "How are you from the opposite side of the planet and your world looks just like mine?"'

'The whole Cyrus family's great. They've always been super friendly to me and very welcoming. I love their family. Her parents are great, they're very friendly people.'
– *Liam Hemsworth*

According to Liam, whilst Miley was on the island she insisted on making several visits to a local cafe called Dr Food, as she'd developed something of a craving for their speciality, the 'Dr Food meat pie with macaroni cheese'. 'The only thing [Miley] really liked there was – we have this place called Dr Food, which has these meat pies,' Liam said. 'They're like chicken pot pies but only with beef. They're pretty much the best thing ever.'

Though they would both have loved to extend their stay on the island, they needed to get back to Los Angeles so that Miley could prepare for her performance at the 2011 Oscars ceremony. And whilst his girlfriend was on stage at the Kodak Theatre, Liam was hobnobbing with the stars at Elton John's viewing party: 'I didn't get a chance to have a chat with him [Elton], but it was my first big event and it was really cool to be inside one of those things and see it all happen, to see all the actors and musicians walking around.'

Opposite: Life is all sunshine for Liam, seen out and about in LA with girlfriend Miley Cyrus in July 2010.

A HOLLYWOOD AFFAIR

'At the end of the day I just try to remember you're there because people want you there; you're there because somebody saw something, and I try to keep that in mind.'
– Liam Hemsworth

According to *Vanity Fair*, when Liam was invited to read for *The Hunger Games* there was only one character he wanted to play: 'It was always for Gale,' he told the magazine. 'I read the script, and Gale definitely felt more right than Peeta.'

Like Jennifer and Josh, Liam is also a fan of *The Hunger Games* trilogy. 'I feel like the books were just written like a movie,' he said. 'You read it and you can just kind of see everything. I read the first book and I loved it. I didn't realise how good the writing was. And then I went in and read with Gary Ross, and that was it.'

Once it was announced that Liam had landed the role of Gale Hawthorne, Chris Hemsworth let it be known that he'd been rooting for his younger sibling: 'I helped him audition. We ran our lines together.' And such was Chris's dedication that he was even prepared to play out the role of Katniss: 'I did. Swear to God. I read that. I put my girly American accent on,' he insisted.

Grabbing a lead role in one of Hollywood's most talked-about film franchises meant Liam's stock was finally rising, but it seemed not everyone was happy for him. For while *The Last Song* had scooped several Teen Choice Awards – with Liam winning the Choice Movie Breakout Male Star Award – the film wasn't particularly well received by the critics, and had performed poorly at the box office. The one

Opposite: Looking up: Liam poses for
a promo shot as his career takes off.

plus the majority of the critics did tend to agree on, however, was Liam's performance. And needless to say, this didn't sit well with Miley. After all, Disney had secured the rights to *The Last Song* as a star vehicle to introduce her to older audiences, and yet it was Liam who was getting all the attention.

It was obvious something would have to give, and shortly afterwards an article appeared in an August 2010 edition of the *National Enquirer* hinting that Miley was envious of Liam's sudden success. Liam was supposedly seen fleeing Miley's house after a massive fallout. The unnamed 'eyewitness', who'd apparently been privy to everything that had occurred that night, also said that Liam was tired of Miley's parents' constant interference.

'I feel like the books were just written like a movie. You read it and you can just kind of see everything. I read the first book and I loved it.'

–Liam Hemsworth

However, another 'Hollywood insider' debunked the rumours of a split and insisted that there was no problem between Liam and Miley. Yet the same insider then proceeded to cloud the issue by saying Miley and Liam were 'still together, even though they're currently far from one another'. But just where Liam and Miley were in geographical terms, the intrepid insider neglected to say.

Over the ensuing weeks the media went into overdrive about the split, and whether Miley was nursing an 'Achy Breaky Heart' like the one her dad Billy Ray had sung about back in 1992. Yet rumours of a reunion started almost the moment Miley arrived back in LA the following month. And confirmation that the warring couple had rekindled their romance came in the most embarrassing form, when they were papped kissing and canoodling in Miley's Mercedes 4x4 in an LA car park. Miley had apparently been pulled over by police for driving whilst talking on her mobile phone and Liam – obviously assuming the coast was clear – had arrived soon afterwards to offer his support.

Opposite: Projecting classic cool in aviator sunglasses, Liam attends the premiere of Thor *in May 2011.*

'What advice would I
offer my younger self?
"You're not cool at all.
Don't think you are,
don't try to be. You're
just not cool."'
– *Liam Hemsworth*

Above: *Liam with Australian model Yolanda Vendy at a party in Melbourne in 2010.*

'I love getting into the physical shape of a character and feeling you're in their skin. I love action movies as long as they have a good story and good characters.'

– Liam Hemsworth

Needless to say, the glossies quickly rolled into action, and in an interview with *OK!* magazine, Miley's half-sister Brandi acknowledged that Miley and Liam were indeed back together: 'Liam is honestly one of the most down-to-earth guys that I have ever met, and he is so easy to get along with,' she said. 'He's a great guy and he makes Miley happy, so that's good.'

Yet when Miley was finally cornered, she refused to give a straight yes or no, and muddied the waters even further by saying: 'I think [love is] someone that's always there to listen. I think the thing people make mistakes about is that they always want to have the answers and they're fixers – and I don't like people trying to fix me.'

Liam proved equally vague when asked if he and Miley were back together after they'd been spotted out and about in LA: 'Who knows? Might be,' he shrugged noncommittally.

However, within weeks of his and Miley's reconciliation, Liam was snapped emerging from a Melbourne nightclub with Australian model Yolanda Vendy.

According to the accompanying newspaper story, Liam and Yolanda had spent the day at the Melbourne Derby Day races before going on

Opposite: 'The best boyfriend': Liam and Miley are still very much an item as they attend the People's Choice Awards in January 2012.

to an aftershow party. When being interviewed at the racetrack earlier in the day Liam – perhaps not surprisingly under the circumstances – made no mention of Yolanda, and instead indicated over his shoulder towards various family members, including his mum and dad and his brother Luke and Luke's wife. But when Yolanda was asked if she and Liam were friends, she coyly set the cat amongst the pigeons by replying: 'If that's what you want to call it.'

Liam opted to maintain a dignified silence on his split with Miley and concentrate on his latest role. For though his character Timmons had been written out of *The Expendables*, Sylvester Stallone had been monitoring Liam's career and reintroduced the character for the 2012 sequel, *The Expendables 2*. And it was obviously worth the wait, as the sequel sees Arnold Schwarzenegger, Chuck Norris, and Jean-Claude Van Damme joining the original film's stellar action-hero cast.

> **'I have the best parents you can have, and they have only ever given me encouragement and support.'**
> **– Liam Hemsworth**

Bruce Willis was signed up to appear in the sequel, and if the rumours currently circulating around Tinseltown are to be believed, Liam has emerged as one of the frontrunners to play Bruce's character's son, John McClane Jr, in the latest of the *Die Hard* franchise: *A Good Day to Die Hard*. According to the *Hollywood Reporter*'s 'insider', Liam was said to be in the process of doing 'chemistry readings' with Willis.

Liam is also reported to be in negotiations to play alongside Anthony Hopkins in Chuck Russell's *Arabian Nights*, a 3-D action adventure romp. 'Yes I am currently in negotiations at the moment,' Liam revealed. 'It's a big epic, fun film. It's about magic, and swords, and action . . . I play the commander of an army, and my king gets killed and I meet up with Sinbad and ask him to help me and come defend my kingdom. He comes back, and we do some sword fighting. I think it's going to be really cool. I love getting into physical shape for a film, it makes me feel more like what the character needs to be.

'We start shooting in September. I love epic films, *Lord of the Rings* and stuff like that. I love getting into the physical shape of a character

Opposite above: Liam hangs with big brother Chris in January 2011. Opposite below: The Hemsworth clan turn out in force to support Chris at the premiere of Thor *in May 2011.*

Opposite: *Liam signs autographs for fans at the Nickelodeon Kids' Choice Awards in Sydney in 2010.*

and feeling like you're in their skin. And I love action movies as long as they have a good story and good characters.

'It's physical and big and magic and epic,' he continued. 'It's a really cool thing to be a part of. I play the prince – the young commander of the army whose king gets killed and he has to go off and sign a treaty with another army but he teams up with Sinbad, who helps him come back and defend his kingdom. It's cool, man.'

Liam was equally thrilled to be working with Chuck Russell: '[Chuck]'s an amazing guy; he's got so many great ideas for the film. He showed me concept art. It'll look amazing. I think he's got a strong vision for the film. He's so enthusiastic about it, and he believes in it so much. And when you have a director like that you know you're in good hands.'

Liam is also believed to currently be in negotiations to play the lead role in Danny Mooney's directorial debut *AWOL*, a Vietnam-era romantic drama based on a true story. The film, which explores the anti-war movement at the University of Michigan, is slated to shoot there in summer 2012.

Other major roles in the offing are *The Power of the Dark Crystal* – a 3-D sequel to the 1982 hit film *The Dark Crystal*, and *Timeless*, a time-travel drama about a young widower attempting to travel back to when his wife was still alive.

Liam's parents, Craig and Leonie, have devoted their working lives to caring for vulnerable children, and when he's away from the cameras Liam serves as the ambassador of the Australian Childhood Foundation. When asked about his involvement with the foundation he said: 'I have the best parents you can have, [and] they have only ever given me encouragement and support. The world is a scary enough place as it is for children. It is important that home should always be a safe place for them.'

'I want to do things that I'm genuinely interested in and believe in. I want to make good stories.'
– *Liam Hemsworth*

When asked if he believed he was a hero to children, he modestly responded: 'I don't know if I'm a hero to children, but I'd like to be. I'd like to be a good role model.'

And what of Liam's future plans – aside from his involvement in *The Hunger Games* trilogy? 'It's almost impossible to plan out what you want to do,' he says. 'You choose things that interest you, what feels right at the time in my career. I want to do things that I'm genuinely interested in and believe in. I want to make good stories. I'd love to do comedies.

'I'd [also] love to do action-y types of films; you know, as long as they're good stories. My favourite actors are Matt Damon and Leonardo DiCaprio and Will Smith – guys like that. I love films that they've done. I love *The Departed*; it's one of my favourite films. I'd love to do a film like that; the acting is just amazing, or a film like *The Bourne Identity*; something that's physical and on edge. I love those kinds of films, and they're the kinds of films I'd love to do.'

GOING FROM PAGE TO SILVER SCREEN

Suzanne Collins says that the main source of inspiration for *The Hunger Games* was the classic Greek myth of Theseus and the Minotaur, which she read as a child. 'I was a huge fan of Greek and Roman mythology,' she explained.

As punishment for displeasing King Minos of Crete, the Athenian King Aegeus agrees to a deal whereby, every nine years, seven Athenian boys and seven Athenian girls are sent to Crete to be eaten by the Minotaur; a monstrous half-man, half-bull creature kept by Minos within a labyrinth. However, after this ritual had taken place a couple of times, Aegeus's son Theseus volunteered to take the place of one of the male youths due to be sacrificed, with the intention of killing the beast. When he arrives in Crete, King Minos's daughter, Ariadne, falls in love with him and, on the advice of Daedalus, the labyrinth's architect, gives him a ball of thread so that he might find his way out of the labyrinth after slaying the Minotaur.

'The story took my breath away, because it was so cruel, and Crete was so ruthless. The message is: "Mess with us and we'll do something worse than kill you – we'll kill your children." And the thing is, it was allowed; the parents sat by powerless to stop it,' Suzanne explained. 'In her own way, Katniss is a futuristic Theseus. I was also heavily influenced by the historical figure Spartacus. Katniss follows the same arc from slave to gladiator to rebel to face of a war.'

Opposite: Jennifer makes waves in a daring, ocean-inspired dress at the People's Choice Awards in January 2012.

A more modern-day stimulus for the storyline came from the world's seemingly never-ending preoccupation with reality TV. Of course, the idea of people being hunted down and killed for the entertainment of the masses has been explored in other films and books, most notably Stephen King's offerings *The Running Man*, which was subsequently made into a film of the same name starring Arnold Schwarzenegger, and *The Long Walk*, which is also set in the near future and has a plotline focusing on 100 teenage boys who participate in a gruelling 'last one standing' walking contest, staged each year by a totalitarian version of the United States of America. Each contestant must maintain a speed of at least four miles an hour to avoid receiving a verbal warning, with three warnings resulting in them being shot, or 'ticketed', to use King's chilling euphemism. (Both stories were first published in 1982 under King's pseudonym, Richard Bachman.)

> **'I was a huge fan of the books before I even really knew about the movies.'**
> *– Jennifer Lawrence*

While some people will no doubt find the thought of kids fighting to the death abhorrent, the concept was first introduced by the Japanese author Koushun Takami in his novel *Battle Royale*, which was first published back in 1999, and made into a film – directed by Kinji Fukasaku – the following year. Indeed, some critics have attacked *The Hunger Games* over its similarities to *Battle Royale*, which is set in an equally dystopian future and sees teenagers fighting to the death on a government-owned island. The *New York Times* opining that 'the parallels are striking enough that Collins's work has been savaged on the blogosphere as a bald-faced rip-off'. However, the paper was willing to concede that there were enough possible sources for the plotline that 'the two authors might well have hit on the same basic set-up independently'.

Of course, Suzanne, who began her career in children's television, and is the first children's author to sell over one million Kindle e-Books, vehemently denies plagiarism and maintains that she'd never even heard of *Battle Royale* – either the film or the 1999 novel – until

Opposite: Jennifer Lawrence poses outside the studio before her appearance on The Late Show with David Letterman *in May 2011.*

after having handed her first book into Scholastic for editing. She says the idea for *The Hunger Games* storyline came to her whilst she'd been channel-surfing one evening at home. Having idly watched a group of hopeful youths competing against each other for some random prize or other on one of the plethora of reality game shows clogging up the network schedules, she'd then inadvertently flicked onto a news channel showing footage of the war in Iraq.

On hearing that Lionsgate Entertainment had purchased the film rights to *The Hunger Games*, American director Gary Ross – having become a devotee of the trilogy after acquiescing to his children's demands that he read the books – might well have considered swimming the Atlantic to plead his case for directing the film. Happily

'Josh totally captured Peeta's temperament, his sense of humour and his facility for language.'
– Suzanne Collins

for him, however, all he had to do was catch a flight to London to meet with producer Nina Jacobson. 'I read the book. My kids turned me on to it, and I went nuts,' he said recently. 'I literally read it and said, "I have to make the movie."'

And Nina – who's subsequently admitted to having been 'very protective of the book', said that, though she already had a line of able directors queuing at her door, she knew from Gary's boyish enthusiasm – coupled with his past directorial successes, such as *Pleasantville* and *Seabiscuit* – that she'd found her director. 'There was a version of the movie that could be made that would in fact be guilty of all of the sins of the Capitol and portray this violence among youth irresponsibly,' she explained. 'If you put the visual wow as your priority over the character of Katniss, you risk making junk food out of something which is anything but. And Gary had a real feel for the balancing act between the epic adventure and the intimate love story.'

While Gary – and his children – were undoubtedly dancing with joy, his being appointed to direct *The Hunger Games* was enthusiastically received by the eighth graders at the Frenship Middle School in Lubbock, Texas, who – under the tutelage of their reading

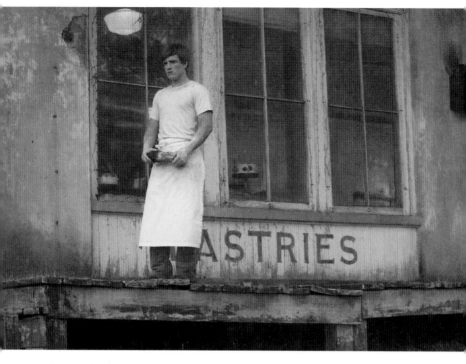

Above: *The boy with the bread: Josh as Peeta in* The Hunger Games.

teacher – each penned a letter offering Gary advice on how best to best proceed. 'So many of them wrote, "Listen, I know this is an action movie and I can't wait to see the action, but please don't lose the heart of the story,"' Gary revealed.

Suzanne – perhaps understandably – was equally anxious that the film version didn't lose the essence of the story, but with Gary having written heart-warming scripts for films such as *Big* and *Dave*, she knew the story was in good hands. 'She [Suzanne] came down to the set, but we also collaborated on the last draft together,' Gary subsequently told *Entertainment News*. 'I wrote a draft, and then Suzanne and I did another subsequent draft, [then we did] the final draft together. She's wonderful. As much as the firestorm or the final action sequences are incredibly riveting and enormous, it's the relationships in the books that are the most moving to me.'

Though Suzanne and Gary had never met prior to their working

'I don't want to be that actor who's like,
"Yeah, man, the role is so me," but it is! I am Peeta.'
– *Josh Hutcherson*

together on the script, their mutual appreciation of each other's work served as a steady platform. 'I was writing the third book [*Mockingjay*], and there was great secrecy about it and no one could know how it ended,' Suzanne said of her involvement in the film. 'But I knew that if the screenplay got off on the wrong foot, you could end up with something by which you could never reach the events of the third book. And since I couldn't reveal information to the film team, I wanted to be around to keep an eye on that.

'Any time you read a book and get attached to the characters, to me it's always a shock when it goes from page to screen and it's not exactly what was in my head or what I was imagining it should be,' she continued. 'So there's always that period of adjustment. But I think we feel so solid about our casting choices, and so thrilled that we've gotten these three young people in those roles, that nothing can really eclipse it.'

Thankfully, Suzanne's anxieties about the characters she'd breathed life into were unfounded, and she subsequently admitted to having been mightily impressed with Gary's draft of the screenplay: 'I was like, "Oh my God, he found the emotional arc to the story!"' she enthused. 'Up to that point, we hadn't really ever cracked that in the script. So I go out to LA, but even then it wasn't until we sat down and started writing together that I was fully on board. When I look at the development of the script, there was the draft I did condensing down the book – what could be cut out of it, and then filling out the backstage stories: because in the film, we have the ability to cut away from Katniss's head.

'The one thing I had never been able clearly to see was not "what's the dramatic question?" – because the dramatic question is fairly forthright: is she going to live? – but it's the emotional arc that exists between Katniss and Peeta. I saw in Gary's draft that it was the first time it had been successfully done as an overall arc. Without it you have a film, you have a story, but you risk losing the kind of emotional impact that the film might have. And I thought, "Well, if they want me in, I have to come." I see it working now.'

'Suzanne and Billy Ray [screenwriter] had done wonderful work, but I told Billy when I began that I would have to put this into my own voice,' Gary explained. 'I wanted to get back as close as I could to the

Opposite: Josh mingles with other up-and-comers at Teen Vogue's *annual Young Hollywood party in September 2011.*

essence of the book; to get inside Katniss's skin and understand how she grows, largely through her relationship with Peeta. I needed to have fresh clay to do that. And then when the draft was done and I got in the room with Suzanne, it was a very, very spontaneous process. I think we had maybe fifteen minutes of discussion, and then we instantly transitioned into writing together seamlessly. She would pitch a line, and I'd pitch the next line, and before you knew it, we had a dialogue scene.

'These are characters and a world that's entirely her invention. Sometimes we'll be working on a scene together and I almost get this giddy feeling because the characters we're talking about are ones she's created. I really haven't had a real writing partner since Anne Spielberg on *Big*, and I feel like I've found that wonderful collaborative electricity again. And now it's really evolved beyond writing because Suzanne is very adroit and savvy about production.

> **'Jennifer was great. She is fantastic; really easy to work with, no drama, really down-to-earth, such a funny girl. I've nothing but good things to say about her.'**
> **– *Liam Hemsworth***

'She has a lot of sophistication about the filmmaking process that isn't just from a writer's perspective out. So we have discussions about costume design, about set design, we talk about casting.'

Suzanne also found working as part of a team rather than on her own strangely invigorating: 'Having spent years in TV rooms I was used to collaborative writing, and if you're with good people it's really fun,' she explained. 'But then with the books, it's been just me talking to me. And I get a little tedious after a while.

'I expect that I will be bouncing back and forth between set and home for most of the production. I definitely want to be there in the early stages for the performers, if anybody has questions about their characters. Sometimes for the writer, the day on set begins and there's not a whole lot for you to do other than hang out at the craft-services table and eat junk food. But there are definitely sequences that I just have to be there to see them film. I have to see the fire. I have to see the bloodbath at the

Opposite: Liam works on his leading man smoulder.

'It didn't feel like filming a movie in the woods, it doesn't have that Hollywood gloss.
– *Jennifer Lawrence*

Above: Into the woods: Jennifer shooting The Hunger Games *on location.*

Cornucopia. I have to see Rue's death. There's a couple of the cave scenes with Peeta and Katniss. Now I'm going to go through it and I'm just going to pick every scene. It's all just a little too exciting to miss.'

While negotiations were underway with Hollywood A-listers such as Donald Sutherland, Stanley Tucci, and Woody Harrelson for some of the supporting roles, Gary, Suzanne and Nina concentrated on finding their three leads.

Nina was already attuned to the growing clamour for an unknown actress to play the role of Katniss. 'I don't think she should be famous. I think that fans want Katniss to belong to them and I understand that,' Nina said at the time. 'And I think that sometimes with people who have a strong "other" identity – as a celebrity, or as a well-known other character – you feel like that person doesn't belong to you and I think that's what fans are looking for.'

Opposite: Jennifer attends the SAGIndie Actors Brunch at the 2010 Sundance Film Festival.

Needless to say, finding the right actress to play the trilogy's central character was absolutely critical, with *Kick-Ass*'s Hit-Girl, Chloë Moretz; *Little Miss Sunshine*'s Abigail Breslin; and Hailee Steinfeld, who received a Best Supporting Actress Oscar nomination for her portrayal of Mattie Ross in the 2010 remake of *True Grit*, being just three of those in the running.

'I understand the fierce and intense feeling the fans have for this movie, [and] we left no stone unturned,' Nina said of the auditions, which fast became the casting competition of 2011. 'But it was Jennifer's gritty performance in *Winter's Bone*, playing a character moved to violence to protect her family [just as Katniss does by standing in her younger sister Primrose's stead] which gave her the edge over the competition. 'It was a lucky break to see her in that role,' she acknowledged.

'Jennifer and I totally hit it off. We're both crazy people – we don't hold anything back, which is really great.'
– Josh Hutcherson

According to Nina, it was Jennifer's audition, the scene where Katniss says goodbye to her family before leaving for the Games, that sealed the deal as her read left everyone in the room in tears. 'You can manipulate appearance, not essence,' she added. 'Jennifer taps the inner life of Katniss.'

For those of you who are as yet unfamiliar with *The Hunger Games* storyline, sixteen-year-old Katniss Everdeen, her mother and twelve-year-old sister, Primrose, live within 'The Seam', as District 12's mining region is known. Her father was killed five years earlier in an underground explosion in the mines, and in those five years she has come to resent her mother for succumbing to the depression caused by the tragedy, which has left her unable to care for Katniss and 'Prim'. Having been thrust into the role of hunter and provider, as well as also having to nurture her younger sister, Katniss has slowly honed the hunting and foraging skills her father taught her on their illicit trips out into the surrounding forest; selling her illegal catches on the district's thriving black market, known colloquially as 'The Hob'.

Opposite: Josh looks relaxed on the red carpet at the 2010 Teen Choice Awards.

One day, having happened upon a rabbit caught in a poacher's snare, twelve-year-old Katniss encounters fourteen-year-old Gale Hawthorne, whose father was also killed in the mine explosion. The two befriend each other and often go hunting together. Katniss shares her father's knowledge about the healing properties of the various herbs that grow in the forest, while in turn, Gale teaches her how to set snares. Though they are breaking the Capitol's strict laws by going out into the forest, the district's Mayor and Peacekeepers willingly turn a blind eye to their activities, and are, in fact, Katniss's best customers at the Hob.

The 'reaping' – when the twenty-four male and female tributes are selected from Panem's twelve districts to compete in the Games – is the most dreaded day of the year. On returning home after selling her and Gale's haul from their latest poaching raid at the Hob, Katniss diverts Prim's mind away from the impending lottery by commenting on her dress. This is the first lottery into which Prim's name has been entered, whereas Katniss, being sixteen, and having accrued four extra entries for taking extra allotments of grain and oil – known as 'Tesserae' – each year, has now been entered a total of twenty times.

> '**Liam's got depth and he's interesting. And at the same time he's natural and he flows.'**
> – *Jennifer Lawrence*

When Prim's name is called out by the Capitol's liaison Effie Trinket as District 12's female tribute, Katniss, without thinking, immediately volunteers to take her sister's place. The district's populace watch in muted silence, and as a mark of respect to a loved one, they all place three fingers to their lips and press outward in a silent salute to Katniss.

Effie is played by Elizabeth Banks, who is perhaps best known for playing the recurring role of Dr Kim Briggs in ABC's long-running, comedy-medical drama series *Scrubs*, and there were times during filming when she feared paramedics would have to be called in: 'We were shooting in North Carolina. It's 100 degrees – like ninety-eight percent humidity. There's, like, 400 extras, or some crazy number. They're all little kids. They're standing in the hot sun,' she explained

Opposite: Liam attends CNN Heroes in December 2011

to *New York Magazine*. 'We felt so badly. We're, like, handing out Popsicles to keep their strength up and they're just dropping like flies.'

Because of the film's subject matter, Elizabeth was also concerned that her character's colourful 'style' – garish clothes and a Day-Glo pink wig – might be misconstrued by audiences: 'You can get away with a lot of things in a book that you can't get away with when you're visually watching kids kill each other,' she said. 'So we just wanted to make sure that she [Effie] didn't look too clownish, and that we honoured the solemnity of what's going on in the book. I wouldn't say we toned it down at all, but it's very specific.'

> **'To Suzanne, Jen is the perfect realisation of the character who is in her head.'**
> – *Gary Ross*

The reaping scene – which Elizabeth was describing – was shot over a sweltering three-day period in a former cotton mill, with 500 extras making up the panicked and miserable inhabitants of District 12. Questions about potential RSPCC violations aside, the scene is arguably one of the most pivotal and moving moments in the film, as it sets in motion an unstoppable chain of events that will forever change Panem. On hearing her sister's name called Katniss screams out, 'I volunteer. I volunteer as tribute,' as the district's Peacekeepers struggle to hold her at bay.

Gary was in complete agreement about Jennifer's appointment: 'You rarely get a tent-pole that has this much emotional depth, this much character to dive into,' he said recently. 'Katniss is incredible. Suzanne did such an amazing job, and painted such a vivid character that I think for me and Jen . . . it was just exciting every day. Not just from a pure filmmaking perspective, but also just in terms of the depth of the acting and exploring the character. Any time you see an actor like this emerge, I think everybody's head sort of snapped, you know? Both from *Winter's Bone*, and other work that she's done, I was just always very aware of her. And then I had a meeting with her, and I was just as impressed, and then she came in and read for us and she sort of blew me away. But I wasn't totally surprised, because I think that an actor like this comes along, you know, once a generation.

'And also, [Katniss is] just such a compelling character, and her struggle and her evolution is so beautiful. You see the character

Above: *Jennifer shows fans she is the perfect Katniss in this still from* The Hunger Games.

emerge and grow and have so much strength. She's a very important character for kids, because she starts off purely in a fight for survival, and by the end of the story she learns there's so much more. [Jennifer] has such command and control of what she's doing, which is a raw, emotional power – it's like looking into a blast furnace at times, and it literally can knock you back in your seat.

'She came in and read for me and it just knocked me out . . . You glimpsed every aspect of the role and the potential of the whole movie. Not only did Suzanne not have an issue with Jen's age, she felt you need someone of a certain maturity and power to be Katniss. This is a girl who needs to incite a revolution. To Suzanne, Jen is the perfect realisation of the character who is in her head.'

Jennifer had first encountered Gary in late 2010 during what she described as 'the height of Oscar season'. 'I was a huge fan of the books before I even really knew about the movies. I met with Gary, and we had a very long, nice meeting before the audition, and then by the time the audition came around, we were familiar with each other.'

Of course, Jennifer was subsequently offered the role of Katniss, and she has since described her response as being 'a mixture of elation – and desperate anxiety': 'I knew that as soon as I said yes, my life would change,' she revealed. 'I walked around an entire day thinking, "It's not too late, I could still go back and do indies [independent films], I haven't said yes yet, it's not too late." [But] I love the story, and if I had said no, I would regret it every day.'

Jennifer then went on to say how much she enjoyed Suzanne Collins's writing: 'I personally like reading the books with the script because it's very rare that you can have an inner dialogue for your character. I think the story is phenomenal. I think it's such an ugly

> **'The cool thing about Katniss is that every fan has such a personal relationship with her, and they understand and know her in a singular way.'**
> *– Jennifer Lawrence*

truth about our world, and it's such an interesting concept of history repeating itself, and the brutality that we all kind of have in us. I love that it's kind of this sick look at our world that's obsessed with reality TV and obsessed with brutality.'

Suzanne was thrilled that Jennifer had signed on to play Katniss, and called her up to say that a weight had now been lifted from her shoulders: 'As the author, I went into the casting process with a certain degree of trepidation,' she explained recently. 'Believing your heroine can make the leap from the relative safety of the page to the flesh-and-bones reality of the screen is something of a creative act of faith. But after watching dozens of auditions by a group of very fine young actresses, I felt there was only one who truly captured the character I wrote in the book.

'I watched Jennifer embody every essential quality necessary to play Katniss. I saw a girl who has the potential rage to send an arrow into the Gamemakers, and the protectiveness to make Rue her ally; [and] who

Opposite: Jennifer's curves caused controversy when she was cast as starving Seam girl Katniss; she makes the most of them here in a figure-hugging dress and funky neon orange belt.

has conquered both Peeta and Gale's hearts even though she's done her best to wall herself off emotionally from anything that would lead to romance. Most of all, I believed that this was a girl who could hold out that handful of berries and incite the beaten-down districts of Panem to rebel. I think that was the essential question for me. Could she believably inspire a rebellion? Did she project the strength, defiance and intellect you would need to follow her into certain war? For me, she did.'

Jennifer said that she readily identified with her character: 'When I was reading about her going to the Capitol was when I was around the Oscar season, and it was just kinda the same feeling of just feeling like I'm putting on these dresses and these uncomfortable shoes and moving around saying what people wanted me to say.

'Katniss is an incredible character. [But] she's a hunter, not a killer; a sixteen-year-old who's being forced into the arena. These kids are killing one another only because if they don't they will die. It's needless, pointless, unjustified violence. It's heartbreaking. When I auditioned, I told Gary, "I understand if you don't hire me, but please remember that after Katniss shoots a bow and kills someone, her face cannot be badass." So there's nothing cool about her. It's not like she looks around the arena and goes, "Yeah, I got this." I think she looks around helplessly, and thinks, I made a promise to my sister that I would survive; now I have to kill in order to do so. These kids are killing one another only because if they don't they'll die. It's heartbreaking.

'She is a young sixteen-year-old girl, but she's also a sixteen-year-old girl whose life is unlike any sixteen-year-old girl of our lifetime, and it was kind of a depth that not anyone her age should have. So it's kind of a balance where she's older than sixteen but she's not.'

Though the internet was raging with debate over the casting of Josh and Liam as Peeta and Gale, once again, Gary, Suzanne, and Nina had no doubts about their choices. 'I was fortunate enough to be in the room with Gary when Josh came in to audition,' Suzanne said recently. 'Three lines into the read [and] I knew he'd be fantastic. Josh totally captured Peeta's temperament, his sense of humour and his facility for language. I'm thrilled to have him aboard.

Opposite: Josh on the red carpet at the 2010 premiere of The Kids are All Right.

'Josh is wise beyond his years, he's sort of mature beyond his years, and there's just such a natural ease to his acting. He's so comfortable.'
– *Gary Ross*

'Gary is amazing. He always has
a billion ideas of what he wants, but has a very
clear perspective also; he just makes it work.'

– Liam Hemsworth

'And you know people may get thrown, say, by the colour of an actor's hair or maybe something physical, but I tell you: if Josh had been bright purple and had had six-foot wings and gave that audition, I'd have been like, "Cast him! We can work around the wings." He was that good. That role is so key to have a boy that can use language. That's how Peeta navigates the world, that's his gift, and Josh was the one who could bring that to life in such a real and natural way.'

Gary was equally enthusiastic about Josh's appointment: 'When I read the book, I thought Peeta would be the hardest role to cast, and I feel so lucky that we found someone who embodies every aspect of such a complex character. I can't wait to work with Josh. He kind of reminds me of a young Jack Lemmon. There's this incredible versatility to him; he's wise beyond his years, he's sort of mature beyond his years, and there's just such a natural ease to his acting. He's so comfortable.

'I remember Suzanne was actually in the room the day Josh came in and read for the first time. After the reading, we looked at each other, we didn't even have to say anything, because we both were like, "Wow, that's it." Literally, he walked out of the room and we high-fived.'

And while Gary was appreciative of the fans' concerns over the castings, he and Suzanne had the advantage of having seen Jennifer, Josh, and Liam audition for these roles. 'I would never judge any role or any actor until I've seen them perform it [and] people should know that we're taking the gravest care in casting these characters,' he said. 'It's not arbitrary. It's of the utmost importance to us that we get the actors who can best bring these characters alive on the screen. Every one of those kids earned those roles by virtue of the auditions they gave. They were all our first choice.'

Josh was somewhat less certain. 'I came in the first time and read a few scenes for Gary and Suzanne, and some of the other producers involved,' he recalled. Yet despite coming away knowing that he'd impressed them both with his reading, he – like the other potential Peetas on the shortlist – was left hanging on tenterhooks.

'Maybe about a week or so, maybe two weeks later, I came in and did a screen test with Jen where I actually read the scenes with her so they could see how the chemistry worked. Both of them [the readings]

Opposite: Liam attends a photo call in March 2010.

felt really great, but as an actor, you just pick apart every single thing that you do, so for me, I was on pins and needles waiting to find out.'

Josh then had another equally agonising wait before being told he'd got the part. 'When I finally found out, my jaw hit the floor. I was so excited.'

In the story, Peeta Mellark – who is also sixteen – is the son of the district's baker. Though he and Katniss attend the same school, his well-to-do family live in the town, whereas Katniss's family live in the poverty-stricken mining community, where everything is coated in a layer of coal dust.

Unbeknownst to Katniss, Peeta has nurtured a secret love for her from the first time he ever heard her sing. And while she is equally ignorant of his name, she remembers how he once saved her family from starvation shortly after her father's death by giving her bread to feed her family. She has never been able to repay his kindness, and is therefore uncomfortable when his name is picked out as the district's male tribute, as she knows she may have to kill him in order to survive.

'Jennifer's just an incredible actress; so powerful, vulnerable, beautiful, unforgiving, and brave.' – *Suzanne Collins*

'There is a brother-sister quality to Jennifer and Josh, which I think is actually great for the dynamic in the relationship,' Gary explained. 'For Katniss, Peeta is an acquired taste. He's not the hot guy that she's into at the beginning. But he's loved her forever, and there's a wonderful kind of close friendship between Jen and Josh that I think serves the Peeta-Katniss relationship so well. It dawns on her slowly that she loves him.'

Josh's confidence largely stemmed from his unshakeable belief that he was the 'Perfect Peeta'. 'I don't want to be that actor who's like, "Yeah, man, the role is so me," but it is! I *am* Peeta: his humility, his self-deprecating humour; his way that he can just talk to anybody in any room,' he enthused over eggs and bacon in an Ashville diner during a break in filming. 'I read the whole series in five days. Bam. Bam. Yes, more. Gimme, gimme. Come on!'

Opposite: Jennifer and Liam pose on the red carpet at the People's Choice Awards in January 2012.

While feeling an empathy with the character was all well and good, Josh still had to convince Gary, Suzanne, and Nina that he was right for the role. And like Jennifer, he had to undergo what he subsequently described as a 'very rigorous auditioning process'.

'I knew a couple of guys in the room, but thankfully not too many of them, so it wasn't too rough,' he recently said of the auditions. 'Honestly, you know, I'm a firm believer that everything happens for a reason . . . I would've kept on truckin' and found the next thing and whatnot. So yeah, I think even though there was a little bit of competition with it, it's definitely a healthy competition. That sort of drive is what keeps all of us actors hungry and wanting more.'

Such was his determination to silence his detractors – convincing audiences everywhere that he'd spent his formative years humping heavy sacks of flour around – that Josh hit the gym and put himself through a rigorous training schedule, adding a creditable fifteen pounds of muscle in one week.

As Katniss is a hunter and provider, Jennifer had to undergo a similarly rigid exercise programme which included lots of running, vaulting and yoga – as well as extensive rock and tree-climbing and hand-to-hand combat courses. And of course, she also had to master the bow. 'I love archery! I really love it. I'm starting to do stunts with the bow and arrow, so I kind of feel like Hugh Jackman,' she enthused. 'It didn't feel like filming a movie. When we were filming in the woods, it doesn't have that Hollywood gloss – it was real snakes, real bears, and really scenes of running up and down a mountain for thirteen hours.'

> '**We had a pretty small crew for being such a giant movie, which was really nice, so when you had these big emotional scenes on set, it's not like there's 150 people standing there and staring at you.**'
> – *Josh Hutcherson*

Two years earlier, Jennifer had appeared in the promotional video for the American indie-rock outfit Parachute's 'The Mess I Made', which was taken from their 2009 album *Losing Sleep*, but according

Opposite: Slam dunk! Josh shows off his sporting prowess in a charity basketball game in 2009.

to *MTV News* she'd made the transition from video extra to being front of house for *The Hunger Games* soundtrack. Whilst taking a break in New York, renowned record producer T Bone Burnett – who was overseeing the film's score – confirmed that Jennifer sings the vocal on the mournful 'Rue's Lullaby'. 'It was beautiful. She did great,' he said. 'She's singing great, [and she's] a killer actor too.'

While her character purposely keeps Peeta at arm's length, away from the camera, Jennifer and Josh developed an immediate rapport. 'Josh is so charming,' Jennifer told *Entertainment Weekly*. 'And when you read the books about Peeta being able to manipulate anybody . . . I mean, Josh could get – well; I don't know a metaphor . . . except for dirty ones. But he's charming, he's sweet, he's down to earth, he's normal. He embodies all of it and brings it all to Peeta . . . he's got all of these great qualities and every single one of them come across in every line he says out loud as Peeta.'

'Josh is charming, he's sweet, he's down to earth, he's normal. He embodies all of it and brings it all to Peeta.'
– *Jennifer Lawrence*

She continued: 'Josh and I are both crazy, and so it's good when we have people that are not crazy to kind of calm us down a little bit, but when Josh and I are together we're so bad for each other. One time Liam, Josh, and I were in [Josh's] room and we were watching some show about crocodiles and then we went screaming about *Avatar* and how upsetting it was and how we couldn't live on Pandora and we couldn't be avatars no matter how we tried, and Liam came running in saying [adopts Australian accent], "Are you guys all right?"'

Indeed, Josh and Jennifer got on so well together on set that Josh decided to have a little fun at his co-star's expense: 'We have this fake dummy on set, this really gnarled-up, scary-looking thing. The other day I put it in her bathroom in her trailer, and she told me she actually peed her pants, she was so scared. I'm sure she's going to pay me back. I'm just terrified because she's someone I can see taking it to the next level, and somebody could get hurt.'

In *The Hunger Games* trilogy, Gale, like Katniss, is rebellious and

Above: *May the odds be ever in your favour: Josh roughs it as Peeta in* The Hunger Games.

goes out of his way to defy the Capitol. And like Peeta, he too has harboured a secret love for Katniss. He is also very protective of her, and whilst she is away participating in the Games, he ensures that her mother and sister want for nothing.

There is, however, a dark side to Gale's nature. And with his ruthless, 'end-justifies-the-means' attitude, he can appear cold-hearted at times – even to Katniss – as he's willing to do anything to overthrow the Capitol, no matter what the cost.

As Gale is a young man of few words, the onus was on finding an actor capable of showing, rather than telling, his character. 'This was accomplished so beautifully in Suzanne's writing, and Liam was able to translate it so naturally to the screen,' Nina said of Liam. 'At the same time, Gale's journey across the three books transforms him, and Liam's performance left no doubt that he would take us there.'

'I'd heard about how popular the books were, but I wasn't quite aware of how dark and gritty the story was,' said Liam, having beaten off stiff competition from the likes of Chris Massoglia, David Henrie,

'I'd heard about how popular the books were, but I wasn't quite aware of how dark and gritty the story was.'
– *Liam Hemsworth*

Robbie Amell and Drew Roy to land the role. 'It started me thinking and asking questions like, "Could something like this actually happen to us one day?" When you think about the fast-growing popularity of reality TV today, and the crazy premise of many of the reality-TV shows that are currently on the air, is it really that far off for us to consider something like this being possible? I think it's a mind-blowing thing to think about.

'For me it has always been about reading great scripts and finding things I relate to, and this was one of those. As an actor, I think you always want your work to do well, and I think that's hopefully what's going to happen. Hopefully this movie does turn out as great as everyone wants it to be, and hopefully we don't disappoint anyone.

'I feel like the books were just written like a movie. You read it and you can just kind of see everything. Right before I went in to read with the director, I read the first book and I loved it. I didn't realise how good the writing was. And then I went in and read with Gary Ross, and that was it.'

Liam loved every minute of filming: 'It was all shot in North Carolina. We shot in a place called Asheville, which is like beautiful, beautiful forests,' he told *Entertainment News*. 'And then part of it we shot all the reaping stuff, which was just crazy – because the reaping in the book and in the script is such an emotional thing for everyone.'

Josh also admitted to finding the reaping scene very emotional, but for different reasons: 'When we did the reaping scene, Gary had a big microphone that he was talking into the entire time,' he explained. 'At the end of the day he asked how many of you guys have read the books? Every single one of those 500 raised their hands and Gary was like, "I want to say something. Thank you first of all. You guys were so amazing. You are not extras, you are all actors. I appreciate your work so much."

'If I was a young guy, first time on a movie set, and I had been trying my best to do what they asked – to be told that would have been such a great feeling. I mean, I loved Gary already, but it made me fall further in love with him.'

Though their characters despise each other in the film, away from the camera Liam and Josh have grown close since their initial meeting on the set of *Red Dawn*, where Josh was working with Liam's brother,

Opposite: Liam practices his sharp-shooting at a display of the latest PlayStation games in February 2011.

Chris. 'On getting the part of Peeta I sent him [Liam] a text: "Dude, we have *The Hunger Games*. I'm so stoked, man, this is awesome!"'

Liam, who'd apparently warned his agent and manager that he'd burn his own house down if the part of Gale had gone to someone else, decided to have a little fun with his new friend and future co-star, and responded saying how happy he was for him, but that he hadn't actually got the part of Gale.

Indeed, the two on-screen protagonists bonded so much on the set that Josh invited Liam to Union to meet his folks – and try his grandmother's fried chicken. There's even talk that they might get an apartment in LA. 'I think it's going to blow people's minds when they see that Peeta and Gale are actually best friends in real life,' Josh chuckled.

Whilst aboard the tribute train to the Capitol, Katniss and Peeta are advised by their mentor, Haymitch Abernathy – a hapless alcoholic who was victorious in the fiftieth Hunger Games, and is the sole living winner from District 12.

Haymitch is played by Woody Harrelson, who, whilst having several major film credits to his name, including *White Men Can't Jump*, *Kingpin*, *Natural Born Killers*, and *2012*, is still perhaps best known for playing simpleton bartender Woody Boyd in the long-running NBC sitcom *Cheers*. 'I think they [Jennifer and Josh] are just marvellous actors. I think they just knocked it out of the park,' Woody enthused to *MTV News*. 'They really just went for it. They worked really, really hard with all that fighting stuff. But just as people, they're about as much fun as it gets. They really are fun. I've never done a sequel before, and I've just signed on to do four [sic] frigging movies, so we're gonna be spending a lot of time together doing the movies, and doing the press, so it's great to love these guys.'

In another pre-release trailer for the film, in which other tributes such as Rue and Cato (played by Amandla Stenberg and Alexander Ludwig respectively) can be seen in the background, Katniss shoots arrows at a target during one of the training sessions for the Games. The wig-wearing Woody, as Haymitch, tells her: 'This is the time to show them everything. Make sure they remember you.' On hearing this, Katniss

Opposite: *Jennifer looks sweet in a simple white dress at the 83rd Oscar nominees' luncheon. She received the Academy nod for her stunning performance in 2010's* Winter's Bone.

'These kids are killing one another only because
if they don't they will die. It's needless, pointless,
unjustified violence. It's heartbreaking.'
– *Jennifer Lawrence*

slowly draws her arm back and releases her arrow. And on seeing the arrow slam into the bull's-eye, we realise – as does Gamemaker Seneca Crane (Wes Bentley) – that Katniss is a force to be reckoned with.

Upon their arrival in the Capitol, Katniss and Peeta are immediately taken to be given a makeover for the Opening Ceremony, when all the tributes are taken through the heart of the Capitol in chariots. Katniss's designated stylist, Cinna, is played by multi-Grammy-winning rocker Lenny Kravitz.

Lenny, who has enjoyed twenty years of mainstream success in music, has also appeared in several films – usually cameo roles as himself – and said in a recent interview with *Rolling Stone* that when Gary called offering him the part of Cinna, he hadn't read any of the *Hunger Games* books and so was unaware of the trilogy's success. However, having subsequently read the books he was 'really excited' to be involved.

> **'You became really close with everyone, and the crew was like a little family, which in my opinion made it more comfortable to give really great performances.'**
> *– Josh Hutcherson*

While there were plenty of seasoned actors lining up for roles in the film, Lenny had a powerful ally fighting his corner, as he explained to the CNN news channel: 'I know [Jennifer] because she did *X-Men: First Class* with my daughter Zoë. She spent a lot of time in my house in Paris when they were filming in London. That was another thing about me. [Gary called and] said, "I heard that Jennifer was in your house all summer and that you were taking care of the kids and they were cooking." I had the whole cast, like six, seven kids in my house on the movie, so I got to know all of them before I had even seen them in action.

'So Jennifer and I ended up becoming friendly. She's really sweet. And then I saw her in *Winter's Bone* and I was like, "Wow. This girl is for real."'

As Katniss is from District 12, Cinna dresses her in a black unitard – complete with matching headdress and cape – to symbolise coal.

Opposite: Josh is his usual, charismatic self in an interview on Good Morning America *in November 2011.*

Above: *One side of the love triangle – Jennifer and Liam as Katniss and Gale in* The Hunger Games.

And as she and Peeta (who is dressed in an identical costume) climb aboard their chariot, Cinna sets alight their capes and headdresses using synthetic fire that doesn't burn. The chariot takes them to the Training Centre, where they will train in an underground gym until the day of the Gamemakers' assessments. This is when each of the tribute's best skills is put to use to attain an assessment score.

At the following day's interviews with oily host Caesar Flickerman (Stanley Tucci), Katniss, having been dressed by Cinna in a stunning bejewelled dress to represent her as being on fire, talks about her stay in the Capitol. When Peeta confesses his love for Katniss to the nation during his interview, Katniss assumes he has done so to curry favour with the sponsors. And while Jennifer said she couldn't have cared less about the dazzling outfits Katniss has to wear for the Gamemakers, she was rather more vocal on the subject of the 'survivalist' clothing: '[As] I'm going to be doing a lot of my own stunts I want to make sure I can run and jump and climb,' she explained. 'The dresses I don't care about. Just put them on me, it's like "Oscar season" again.'

In a recent post-production interview with *Seventeen* magazine, Josh admitted that playing 'lovesick puppy Peeta' to Jennifer's 'cold-hearted Katniss' came pretty easy to him: 'I feel like every relationship I get into ends up being like that! I'm someone who can fall in love at the drop of the hat. My parents raised me to be very accepting of other people, so because of that, I feel like I might be overly accepting of girls. If a girl shows any interest, I'm like, "Yes! I love you, you're amazing!"'

When asked who would win if he and Liam had to fight it out to the death over a girl, he chuckled: 'Let's be honest, his Australian accent kills it. It's an unfair advantage! I'd give the lady-points straight to Liam. Liam is epic, man.' And of course, when the same question was put to Liam he was equally diplomatic: 'Josh is a pretty

'You have a whole other level, which is the chemistry between the characters. We can tell you it's there but you'll have to see it for yourself.'
– *Gary Ross*

charismatic dude, so he'd probably win. 'I'm not that good at talking to girls. Honestly, he's persuasive, I listen to him talk a lot and he's smart, he's funny . . . he could convince me to do anything!'

Jennifer said in a recent interview with the *Washington Post* that she didn't think there was a means-tested way for an actor to prepare for the expected media attention for a high-profile film such as *The Hunger Games*. 'It's kind of scary, to be honest,' she confessed. '[But] I love the movie and I love the books, and I didn't want to just turn away because I was scared [of the scrutiny].'

And Josh was equally pragmatic when asked about his potentially career-changing role: 'I know it's going to be a big change. But I think if you go about it in the right way, you can still have your privacy. You've got to just keep on trucking and make sure you're always being true to yourself. Which is so funny, because – God bless America! – that's exactly what Peeta would say.'

Winning means fame and fortune. Losing means certain death. The Hunger Games have begun. May the odds ever be in your favour.

British Library Cataloguing in Publication Data

O'Shea, Mick.
  Beyond District 12: the stars of The hunger games.
  1. Hemsworth, Liam, 1990–Juvenile literature.
  2. Lawrence, Jennifer, 1990–Juvenile literature.
  3. Hutcherson, Josh–Juvenile literature.4. Motion
  picture actors and actresses Biography–Juvenile
  literature. 5. Hunger games (Motion picture)–
  Juvenile literature.
  I. Title
  791.4'3'028'0922-dc23

ISBN-13: 978-0-85965-487-6

Cover and book design by Coco Wake-Porter
Printed in Great Britain by Scotprint

Acknowledgements: Thanks to Sandra, Laura and Tom
at Plexus for their assistance in my bringing the book
in on time, Rupert Tracy, and Jackie and Richard at
P-PR. Thanks also to Tasha 'Bodacious Babe' Cowen
and Shannon 'Mini-Hepburn' Stanley, for keeping
the tea flowing, and putting up with my mood-swings
and frustrations when occasionally stumbling over the
dreaded writer's block, Paul Young (not the singer) Lisa
'T-bag' Bird, Johnny Carroll, Fi Bartlett and the twins,
Debbie Mustapha, Zoe Johnson-Meadows, Martin and
Angela Jones, Phil and Nic Williams.
  Jennifer Lawrence, Josh Hutcherson and Liam
Hemsworth have given interviews to many
newspapers, magazines, and websites, and these
have proved invaluable in chronicling their lives
and careers. The author and editors would like to
give special thanks to: *Vanity Fair*, *Elle* magazine,
The New Yorker, *New York Magazine*, *Teen Vogue*,
Flare magazine, *Seventeen* magazine, *Woman's
Day* magazine, *Dolly* magazine, *OK!* magazine,
Entertainment Weekly, *J-14*, *People* magazine, *US
Weekly*, the *New York Times*, the *Louisville Courier-
Journal*, the *Washington Post*, *The Hollywood Reporter*,
the *Cincinnati Enquirer*, the *Chicago Tribune*, the
Lexington Herald-Leader, the *Herald Sun* (Melbourne),
the *Daily Telegraph* (Australia), the *National
Enquirer*, the *Globe and Mail* (Toronto), CNN.com,
MTV.com, thehungergamesmovie.com, thehob.
org, mockingjay.net, entertainmentnews.co.uk,
cinemablend.com, cellebuzz.com, moviefone.com,
adelaidenow.com, dailystar.com, clevvertv.com,
jennifer-lawrence.org, imdb.com, popsugar.com.au,
deadline.com, aceshowbiz.com, hollywoodlife.com,
accesshollywood.com.
  Cover photographs by: Getty Images/ WireImage/
Stringer; Rex Features/ BEI/ Photowire. We would
like to thank the following for supplying photographs:
Marcel Thomas/ Getty Images, Kevin Mazur/
WireImage/ Getty Images; Jon Kopaloff/ FilmMagic/
Getty Images; Alessandra Benedetti/ Corbis;
Alessandra Benedetti/ Corbis; Michael Buckner/
Getty Images; Angello Picco/ Rex Features; c.TBS/
Everett/ Rex Features; Startraks Photo/ Rex Features;
c.Wild Bunch/ Everett/ Rex Features; Lester Cohen/
WireImage/ Getty Images; Frazer Harrison/ Getty
Images; c.Roadside/Everett/ Rex Features; c.Roadside/
Everett/ Rex Features; Steve Granitz/ WireImage/
Getty Images; Alexandra Wyman/ WireImage/
Getty Images; c.Everett Collection/ Rex Features;
c.Paramount/ Everett/ Rex Features; Sipa Press/ Rex
Features; John Shearer/ Getty Images; Dominique
Charriau/ WireImage/ Getty Images; c.20thC.Fox/
Everett/ Rex Features; Murray Close/ Moviepix/
Getty Images; Jeff Kravitz/ FilmMagic/ Getty Images;
Donna Ward/ Getty Images; NBCUPHOTOBANK/
Rex Features; Startraks Photo/ Rex Features; Jason
Merritt/ FilmMagic/ Getty Images; SGranitz/
WireImage/ Getty Images; John Sciulli/ WireImage/
Getty Images; c.20thC.Fox/ Everett/ Rex Features;
c.Columbia/ Everett/ Rex Features; Lisa O'Connor/
Zuma/ Corbis; E. Charbonneau/ WireImage/ Getty
Images; Jun Sato/ WireImage/ Getty Images; Kevin
Winter/ Getty Images; c.Columbia/ Everett/ Rex
Features; c.BuenaVist/ Everett/ Rex Features; Stephen
Shugerman/ Getty Images; c.20thC.Fox/ Everett/
Rex Features; Jeff Vespa/ WireImage/ Getty Images;
Patrick Rideaux/ Rex Features; c.New Line/ Everett/
Rex Features; Universal/ Everett/ Rex Features; Frank
Trapper/Corbis; c.Focus/ Everett/ Rex Features;
AFP/ Stringer/ Getty Images; Brendon Thorne/
Stringer/ Getty Images; Serge Thomann/ WireImage/
Getty Images; James Devaney/ WireImage/ Getty
Images; Luis Ascui/ Getty Images; George Pimentel/
WireImage/ Getty Images; Mark Metcalfe/ Stringer/
Getty Images; c.W.Disney/ Everett/ Rex Features;
c.W.Disney/ Everett/ Rex Features; BDG/ Rex
Features; Lester Cohen/ WireImage/ Getty Images;
Lucas Dawson/ Getty Images; Broadimage/ Rex
Features; Graham Denholm/ Stringer/ Getty Images;
Matt Baron/ BEI/ Rex Features; Startraks Photo/
Rex Features; Lionsgate Films/ Image Net; Donato
Sardella/ WireImage/ Getty Images; Fred Hayes/
Getty Images; Lionsgate Films/ Image Net; Frank
Trapper/ Corbis; Jim Smeal/ BEI/ Rex Features;
Lionsgate Films/ Image Net; Henry Lamb/ Photowire/
BEI/ Rex Features; Theo Wargo/ WireImage/ Getty
Images; Theo Kingma/ Rex Features; Stewart Cook/
Rex Features; Startraks Photo/Rex Features; Lionsgate
Films/ Image Net; Ray Tamarra/ Getty Images;
Lionsgate Films/ Image Net.
  Every effort has been made to acknowledge and
trace copyright holders and to contact original sources,
and we apologise for any unintentional errors which
will be corrected in any future editions of this book.